Better Time Management

JACQUELINE ATKINSON

Thorsons
An Imprint of HarperCollins*Publishers*

For my brother, Edward,
and for Per,
who both need it,
with love.

The quotation from Christopher Fry is from *The Lady's Not For Burning*, 1948, and used by permission of Oxford University Press.

Thorsons
A Division of HarperCollins*Publishers*
77–85 Fulham Palace Road
Hammersmith, London W6 8JB

Published by Thorsons in 1992
10 9 8 7 6 5 4 3 2

© Jacqueline Atkinson 1992

Jacqueline Atkinson asserts the moral right to
be identified as the author of this work

A CIP catalogue record for this book
is available from the British Library

ISBN 0 7225 2611 3

Typeset by Harper Phototypesetters Limited,
Northampton, England
Printed in Great Britain by
HarperCollinsManufacturing Glasgow

CONTENTS

INTRODUCTION

There is more to time management than simply being better organized or working faster. Most approaches to time management are mechanistic — sort out your goals, get yourself organized with a particular 'system' and with a bit of self-discipline your problems are solved. Somehow it is never that easy. To understand why you have a problem managing your time you need first to understand what the problem is (to find a more specific answer than there's 'too much to do'), then begin to look at why you have the problem. Successfully solving the problem means not just making a difference now, or even for the next few weeks, but finding ways of managing your time that will last forever.

This is accomplished by examining the behavioural and psychological aspects of time management as well as the more practical organization of time. You must look at the habits, attitudes and beliefs that have led to the development of time management problems. Unless these are examined and dealt with, no externally applied 'system' will completely work — it is more like trying to wallpaper over the cracks. Do you really have too much to do? How much do you have to do? How much do you want to do? How much of this is your own making? Where do the demands on your time come from? How much is too much?

Throughout this book the approach taken will be to examine your behaviour and attitudes to find an individual approach which suits you, rather than applying one prescriptive system. Just as there are many reasons why individuals have time management problems, and many ways this can show itself, there are many different solutions. Only part of the system you will eventually work out for yourself is determined by the job you do. Your personality, upbringing, beliefs, attitudes and social context, the skills you have and your aesthetic sense, all matter. This is not as daunting as it sounds if you approach the problem – and the solutions – in a systematic manner. And certainly not as daunting as trying to work to someone else's set of rules that don't quite apply to you. There are some basic building blocks that are useful to everyone (see, for example, Chapter 3 on goals) but do you really expect the same answer to suit you, your neighbour, the woman in the next office block, the man on the Clapham omnibus . . . ?

Time management isn't only for your working life, it also applies to your personal, social and family life. Time management is for everyone, men and women, young and old, in work or not working, in any type of job. Time management is about helping you get out of life what you want, and, in so far as it is possible, doing things the way you want. It is about having time to enjoy what you do as well as getting through what you have to do. Or, at least, that's my perception of it. On my deathbed I want to look back not just at things I've done, or things I've achieved, but I also want to feel that I've enjoyed my life, rather than endured it. If you want other things that's your choice entirely. It is not for me to set your goals for you, only to help you to the best way of achieving them.

⌛ PART 1

Time
and You

1

THE NATURE OF TIME

Ah, fill the Cup: — what boots it to repeat
How Time is slipping underneath our feet:
Unborn TO-MORROW, and dead YESTERDAY,
Why fret about them if TO-DAY be sweet!
EDWARD FITZGERALD

A common sense view of time tells us that one person has the same amount as another, that it is unambiguously measurable, it is independent of space, and it moves inexorably forward. Aristotle would have been happy with this view of time; so would Sir Isaac Newton. Not so that remarkable Professor of Mathematics, Stephen Hawking. As he points out in his bestseller, *A Brief History of Time*, common sense notions are fine in their place, when they deal with apples or even planets that travel comparatively slowly, but our understanding of time doesn't work when we are dealing with things which travel at or near the speed of light. Professor Hawking's theorising may lead him to conclude that there is no beginning or end to time, indeed that the universe has no start and no finish, but his musings need not detain us. None of us is likely to travel at the speed of light in the near future, and so our notions of time hold good for our practical purposes, bound as they are by our social conventions.

For us there are twenty-four hours in a day, seven days in a week. In parts of Africa and Central America there are five-day market weeks. The Incas had an eight-day week; the Yoruba have a sixteen-day market week. But the most complicated of all are the Kedangese of eastern Indonesia. They have ten kinds of week, ranging in length from one to ten days, each with its own name and all running simultaneously. But however we measure our time, days move forward — a minute passed is gone forever. So why do we sometimes act as though we can change the laws of the universe? Why do some people seem to have more time than others? Why do we assume some have more than others? Patients waiting for appointments are expected to have lots of time; doctors are always short of it. We organise our days, or others organise them for us. Why do we think that the answer to our problem is 'more time'?

Part of the challenge of learning to manage your time is to investigate your personal relationship with time. Why are some people habitually late and others always early? The clock tells us one minute is as long as another, so why does time sometimes fly, sometimes drag? As we get older the years get shorter. And naturally so. We measure time on a personal scale as well as by our watches, and tend to identify the centre of the universe with ourselves. At 4 years old one year is a quarter of our life and next birthday seems forever away. At 40 a year is only one-fortieth of our life and 50 seems round the corner. A year, from our perspective, does get shorter.

When faced with the problem of too much to do and too little time to do it in there are alternatives to needing 'less to do' or 'more time'. If you had an extra hour a day, what would you do with it? Think of this as your first exercise in managing your time. If you chose to work during that extra hour would it solve your 'too much to do' problems, or would it make little difference? Would you choose to take on yet another project because of that extra hour? Are you going to catch up on sleep, spend the time with your family or slump in front of the television?

A central part of time management is not just looking at what you currently do, or even what you have to do, but at what you want to do. In the following chapters it will be as important to look at your personal attitudes to time, the things you want to do as well as the things you have to do, as we examine the more mechanistic aspects of time management.

There is a tendency among journalists, posing as social historians, to label decades, to point to social trends. If the 'entrepreneurial eighties' prized individualism and material success, self-control and self-discipline, then they also brought new concepts like 'hurry sickness' to the fore, and promoted the workaholic. Independence, self-sufficiency and material success can be liberating, but they can also be emotionally sterile.

'Quality time' was an expression coined to con those people who hardly saw their children, partners or friends that it didn't matter. The amount of time wasn't the issue, so long as the few minutes they could tear themselves away from their job was meaningful. The underlying message was that if you weren't doing something useful, worthwhile, productive, or deeply enjoyable, you were wasting time. We need to ask ourselves whether our children would like to see us for more than half an hour a day, even if some of that time we're doing nothing more than watching television with them?

We need to ask ourselves whether it is possible to be productive all the time? And even if it is possible, is it desirable? Even relaxing can become serious work when improving your technique, be it yoga or meditation for example, takes over from the real purpose. What about the pleasure of sloth? Not apathy or tiredness, but occasionally taking time out to laze and do nothing very much but enjoy the freedom of no deadlines, no priorities, no list of 'things to do'. For some people the very idea puts them in a mild (or not so mild) panic. Why? Why do they need to be busy, busy, busy?

Faster can mean better. But is this the case if it means losing a process you enjoy? Why should you always want to do everything faster, particularly, for example, when you are enjoying a leisure activity? Why force yourself to work directly onto a word processor if you enjoy writing in long-hand first? Do the benefits outweigh what you lose?

Some of the harder, faster norms of the 1980s are disappearing, but there is still enough hangover from our social conditioning to affect many people who see themselves as having time management problems. If time management is about doing what *you* want, to achieve your own goals, it is not for me to tell you what those goals are or should be. I do want, however, to help you think about both the external and internal factors which contribute to your sense of time and its use.

Work Ethic

We work not only to produce but to give value to time.
FERDINAND VICTOR EUGÈNE DELACROIX

The Protestant work ethic lies behind many time management problems. It tells us the more we work, the harder we work, the more we deserve to achieve, to have. It tells us also that if we haven't worked for something we don't deserve it (and thus it may/will be taken away) or it isn't worth having. So many in our society are caught up in a trap that has all the physical, psychological and, indeed, spiritual discomfort of the work ethic, with none of the spiritual solace. This leads people to believe they have to be doing something useful all the time. They are the people who never read fiction, only books that will extend their knowledge, and usually work-related knowledge. They are less likely to have friends, more likely to have an address book full of business acquaintances, people who are, or who might be, useful to know. Visits to exhibitions, galleries, theatres or concerts are more about impressing people than enjoyment or relaxation.

How strong is the work ethic in you?

- Do you feel uncomfortable if you're not doing something all the time? That relaxing is a waste of time?
- Do you feel guilty if you're not doing something useful? Do you stretch the definition of 'useful' to deal with your guilt feelings and anxiety?
- Do you measure your worth (and others') by how much you've achieved?
- Do you measure enjoyment by how much you've achieved? Do you see spending time socializing as a waste? Do you spend time with your children/friends and then ask yourself what you have to show for it?
- Do you feel you only deserve something if it has cost you a lot of time/energy/effort?
- Does having nothing to do produce a sense of panic?
- Do you spend time justifying what you do to yourself and/or

others to somehow make it 'count'?
* Do you find yourself muttering 'time is money'?

A strong sense of the work ethic need not be a bad thing, but like so much in life, it can cause problems if taken to extremes. Two problems which can be related to the work ethic are 'hurry sickness' and workaholism.

Hurry Sickness

The natural pace of life in an agrarian society is quite different from our speeded-up life in an 'information society' where everything from fast-foods to office technology demands instant responses. McDonalds shows us the pace: two minutes in the queue, one minute at the counter — with staff aiming to get customers moving faster than they would normally.

We measure the pace of life by interruptions, or the length of time between interruptions. In other words, the pace of our lives is determined by the frequency with which others demand our attention. Think of the difference in satisfaction between watching a movie without commercials and one where your concentration is interrupted and your attention demanded by constant breaks, whether you like it or not.

Hurry sickness is a phrase used to describe people with an overdeveloped sense of time urgency. American cardiologists Meyer Friedman and Ray Rosenman first identified what they termed the 'Type A' personality in the 1950s. The term is still a popular and useful label for a person who might be described as 'hard-driving', who might, and probably does, suffer from hurry sickness. The links between Type A behaviour and heart disease remain controversial; recent research points to hostility and low self-esteem as crucial factors in Type A people developing health problems. And not everyone who is Type A has a problem: some people love the constant pressure, and apparently thrive on it. However, some people love it but still crack up, physically or psychologically. Others feel that it is a type of behaviour thrust on them by the climate of the times, their company's expectations or even their own boss's managerial style.

Problems associated with Type A behaviour can be seen generally in the form of stress, but where it is particularly related to hurry sickness the person has a sense of time slipping away from his or her control and any period of activity will cause extreme agitation. People with hurry sickness *have* to be on the go all the time. Women who find it hard to overcome the early social conditioning which encourages them to hide other Type A characteristics, such as aggressiveness, egocentricity or even ambition, will show their Type A tendency through time urgency.

How is your sense of time urgency?

- Do you speak quickly, running words and sentences together?
- Do you interrupt people, hurry them up, finish their sentences for them?
- Do you eat fast, even to the point of indigestion? Do you want to leave the table as soon as you've finished, not waiting for others?
- Are all your movements rapid? To the point of being clumsy?
- Do you walk fast, to the point of bumping into things and people? Do you get hot, bothered and out of breath?
- Do you sweat a lot, particularly on your forehead and upper lip?
- Are you impatient? Irritable? Are you aware of this?
- Do you hate queuing or waiting just about more than anything else?
- Do you try to do two or more things at the same time? All the time? Even when they require concentration?
- Do you define a sense of urgency as exciting? Exhilarating? Motivating? As a way of knowing you're getting something done?
- Do people keep telling you to slow down? Do they make comments about blood pressure/having a heart attack/suffering a stroke? Do they get tired and impatient with your 'go, go, go' attitude?

Workaholism

Workaholic is a word frequently applied to people who work too hard and too long, even when they are successful. It is a quality that is often admired: people refer to themselves self-deprecatingly as a workaholic, whilst being secretly proud of the fact, knowing that it is a virtuous failing. Hard work is generally respected in a society strong on the work ethic. In Japan a word has been coined for death by overwork — *karoski*. Although the government refuses to acknowledge its existence, in 1989 more than 1,300 families sought information on filing claims against companies for death of family members from overwork. And one claim has been upheld in the courts.

Working long hours is not necessarily a problem. If you have no other demands on your time, such as family obligations, if it makes you happy and your health isn't suffering, you might argue, 'Why not?' It is potentially a problem when work becomes all-pervasive, all-consuming. It becomes an end in itself rather than a means to an end and the person closes off everything but work. Workaholics don't realize they have nothing but work.

The term workaholic obviously has overtones of addiction, but the idea of being 'addicted' to work can be attractive. It is more useful, however, to look at working long hours as a habit which started for one, or more, of a variety of reasons and continues for one, or more, of a variety of reasons. We will be examining such reasons later. For now, it is enough to consider whether you have a workaholic problem or tendency.

- Do you feel guilty about the amount of time you spend working? because you're neglecting your family? other interests?
- Do you work in secret? Do you work when you're supposed to be doing something else? Do you work during your 'free' time, or on holiday?
- When you're on holiday do you leave a number at work where you can be reached? Do you telephone your work to check up on things?

- Do you think about work most of the time? Does this cause you sleep problems?
- Once you start working do you find it hard to stop?
- Do you make excuses, to yourself and others, to justify the amount of time you spend working?
- Is your lifestyle dictated by your work? Is your family's lifestyle dictated by your work?
- Do you sometimes work straight through the night or weekend? even when it's not a life-or-death emergency?
- Do you take on work which isn't your responsibility? that is 'below' you (in terms or status or ability)? Do you look for things to do?
- Do you feel insecure when faced with 'free time'? when your diary is empty?
- Are you taking longer to achieve the same amount of work? Is it harder to maintain standards?
- Do people tell you you're working too hard? Do you enjoy this, or pretend not to hear?
- Does the amount of time you spend working cause arguments with your partner, or your children?
- Would you rather work than spend time with your partner, children or friends?

Inflexibility

Flexibility is a quality prized in most situations. It means you can tolerate ambiguity (up to a point) without becoming stressed, you can assimilate conflicting information without needing to force it into a coherent whole or neglect the parts which don't fit. Flexible people adapt to the situation, and learn new skills as and when (often before) necessary. The flexible person is able to explore all kinds of solutions to a problem, the obvious, the not-so-obvious and the downright unlikely. If you are flexible you can drop one line of thought to follow another, rearrange priorities, and shift gear. All of this is highly laudable behaviour and, from a time management perspective, useful.

Flexibility is only a problem when it becomes 'butterfly' behaviour, and you flit from task to task without finishing anything.

The reverse of flexibility can be, however, a major time management problem. Inflexibility means change worries you, you're unhappy about abandoning old habits – ways of thinking and behaving, things or even people. You like order, routine, tradition. In its place this can be appropriate: people who are less flexible often pay close attention to detail and work through a series of logical steps. They can be reluctant to leave one task to start another, no matter how important. Their motto is 'I've started so I'll finish.' This becomes a problem when your sense of logic or view of the problem is challenged and you can't handle it. It may also make you less able to solve novel problems, or move to newer types of solutions.

Is inflexibility holding you back?

- Do you plan activities carefully, even trivial ones? Do you have schedules you stick to, come what may? Do you get disproportionately upset if something happens to disrupt your plan/schedule?
- Do you believe in 'a place for everything and everything in its place'? Do you get upset when people don't put things back exactly as you left them? Do you dislike lending things?
- Are you always punctual? Over-early? Do you get upset when people are late (even if they have a good reason)? Do you get upset if you have to cancel an appointment?
- Do you have a set routine when you do certain tasks and which is not set by external demands? Do you get upset if you can't stick to this?
- Do you find it hard to make a decision when faced with the unexpected? Once you've made a decision do you worry about whether it was the 'right' one?
- Do you do things 'out of habit' even when it is not necessary?
- Do you miss opportunities because you didn't act quickly enough at the time?
- Do you get annoyed with other people for not falling in with

your plans/sticking to your schedule/doing what you want?
- Do you avoid taking risks whenever possible?

What Do You Want Time For?

This takes us back to the question I posed earlier — if you had more time what would you do with it? Before moving on to the more structured exercises which follow, begin to ponder on some of the questions below. There are no right answers, and often there are no easy answers. They are the sort of questions to come back to at spare moments, the sort you get flashes of inspiration about at the oddest times. Use these questions to expand your horizons in thinking about time.

- What do you regret not having done in your life so far?
- What do you want to achieve more than anything else?
- If you had an extra hour a day, what would you do with it?
- Which is more important to you, your work or your family?
- How do you want to feel when you retire?
- What activities give you the most pleasure?
- What activities give you the best sense of achievement?
- If you could do anything, what would it be?

Time is described in myriad ways by poets, philosophers and scientists, but stop, just for a moment, and think about the way you visualize time.

Do you see it as a straight line, with a one-way arrow, forward? Maybe you see it as a series of loops, as your life goes through cycles. Maybe it is a wavy or jagged line, or a series of dots and dashes indicating that it apparently moves at different speeds. Is it a big black hole into which everything is sucked and nothing ever reappears — at least in this universe? Or is it a box in which you are trapped in the present, with the past and the future forever inaccessible? Tennyson described time as 'a maniac scattering dust', and Shakespeare speaks of the 'whirligig of time' bringing his revenge. What expressions do do you use most about time?

Do you talk of 'wasting time', 'saving time', 'losing time', 'killing time', 'time flying' or 'time dragging'? When you're pressured and overworked it's all too easy to see time as your enemy, but you need to view it as your friend. You can't 'save' it, like money; you can't cheat it; the only time you can beat it is when conducting music. You have twenty-four hours a day and only God knows how many years. Stop playing games with time and treat it honestly and you will find it treats you more fairly. Time management is about planning for the future; it is also about living today.

> *While we're talking, time will have run meanly on: pick today's fruits, not relying on the future in the slightest.*
>
> HORACE

2

WHY TIME MANAGEMENT?

A desperate disease requires a desperate remedy.

GUY FAWKES

Just as you can't mend something, nor improve it, until you know how it works, you can't begin to solve your time management problems until you know why you've got a problem and where your time goes.

What Sort of Problem Have You Got?

Write down a list of *all* the reasons *why* you think you have a time management problem. Do this before you read any further.

How many items have you got? Some people will only have a couple. Others of you will have a list running to dozens. This isn't necessarily a measure of how great your problem is, so much as an indication of the way you see it, and probably what you think you could do about it. If you've only written down a few items they will probably be 'big' reasons, like 'too much to do'. In such cases, you will have to learn how to break this down to find out what 'too much to do' really means. Try and expand this now, although we'll come back to it in succeeding chapters.

Now look at your list and write down by the side of each item whether it is an internal or personal reason, or whether it is external — to do with other people or things.

The personal category includes:

- Organizational problems, such as:
  - 'I spend too much time on trivial things'

- 'I never finish one thing before starting another'
- 'I can't keep track of things'
- Psychological issues such as:
  - 'I've no self-discipline'
  - 'I can't say no'
  - 'I'm interested in too many things'
- Difficulties in your relationships with other people such as:
  - 'I don't delegate enough'

The external category includes:

- Relating to other people such as:
  - 'Too many interruptions'
  - 'Other people are unreliable'
- Things relating to the company or institution for which you work such as:
  - 'It takes a week to get a simple decision'
  - 'There aren't enough staff'

The last category relates to social or cultural norms which you feel put pressure on you:

- To do particular things
- To fulfil roles in a certain way (a common issue for working mothers)
- You feel you're being judged by a set of social criteria you don't agree with

In Chapter 7 we'll see how these different types of problems are interrelated and how much they have to do with certain attitudes and beliefs you hold.

Where do most problems come from? It is a good thing if you've got a list with a fair number of problems related to yourself because you have some understanding of what is going on and the part you play. If, however, you relate all your problems to other people or the company, you may need to reassess some of your thinking before you begin to solve your problems successfully.

Now, I am not for a moment suggesting that all your difficulties in time management stem from yourself. Many people are in jobs which, for whatever reason, demand more than they can give, or more than is reasonable. Often this stems from cutbacks and staff shortages which have led to additional tasks being grafted on to a job. Or the job itself has changed and new things have been added, but nothing lost. Sometimes these new tasks are things you know little about, or do not have the requisite skills to perform. The philosophy and political spirit of recent years seemed to demand that everyone work longer and harder.

It is true that some people are in an impossible position with respect to what is required of them. It is too easy, however, to hide behind this and to say the problem is 'out there', that it isn't to do with you. For many people, it's a bit of both. Yes, your job may have changed. Yes, you may feel under pressure to do more, but in most cases there are things you do which contribute to the problem. And, in finding solutions, this is an important aspect. Changing yourself can be difficult, but changing other people is harder still. We will return to issues involved in change in Chapter 8. For now it is enough that you begin to sort out what hinders your time management.

In the introduction I said that the solution would not be the same for everyone, and analysing where your problems lie is the first step to developing a personal style of time management. You will not be able to deal with everything at once. Solutions can be short-term, long-term or preventive. Some short-term solutions can be quick, comparatively easy ways of dealing with parts of a problem, or handling sudden overload, others are holding measures while you develop a long-term strategy. Long-term strategies have a way of becoming preventive, and this is even better.

The chart on page 25 provides an outline in which you can gradually come to see where your problems lie and what you can do about them. Some things you may realistically decide you can do nothing about, but living with them may be easier if you get more control over other parts of the equation. I'm not suggesting you fill in the squares so much as think about where problems and solutions belong in such a scheme which gives you a broader perspective on what can be a narrow vision of time management. It is a tool to keep coming back to, a reminder of issues that are resolved and still to be resolved.

You are not going to solve your time management problems overnight, or even in a week. It has taken you some time to reach the point you're at now — ten, twenty, thirty years? To expect to change ingrained habits immediately is unrealistic, just as it is to assume you can immediately see what the whole problem is. Changing always takes time.

Problems / Solutions	Personal	Other People	Institutional	Social/Cultural
Short-term				
Long-term				
Prevention				

Strategy For Change

Where Does Time Go?

O! call back yesterday, bid time return.
WILLIAM SHAKESPEARE

In the next chapter we'll concentrate on what you *want* to do with your time; for the rest of this chapter we'll look at what you *actually* do with it. If you're going to change anything you need to know what is going on now. The chart on page 26 is a list of activities you may find yourself engaged in during an average week, with space for you to add in other areas that are important to you. Now, in Column 1 estimate how much time you spend in each activity (go for a gut feeling rather than trying to work it out). Note that there are 168 hours in a week — if necessary adjust your total down to meet that. If your total doesn't reach 168 hours don't worry. In Column 2 enter the amount of time you would like to spend on each activity; again it has to total 168 or less — planning for a longer week isn't allowed!

Before you begin to compare these you need some information to fill in Column 3 and this brings us to the time log.

	1	2	3
• Working (in total)			
• Aspects of work important to you			
. . .			
. . .			
. . .			
. . .			
. . .			
. . .			
. . .			
. . .			
• Chores/housework			
• Childcare			
• With your family			
partner			
children			
. . .			
• With friends			
• Relaxing			
• Hobbies/leisure interests			
• Sleeping			
• . . .			
• . . .			

Use of Time

Time Log

If you want the present to be different from the past, study the past.

BARUCH SPINOZA

I'm not going to pretend that keeping a time log is the most fun pastime I can think of but it does have many important uses. It gives you baseline data about what you do, when, where, a feel for interruptions, where time gets lost, and how long things take. You will come back to it on a number of occasions over succeeding chapters so it is worth doing properly. The best layout is shown on page 28. Either copy this page or make your own.

Most people will keep the time log for their working day only, but if your working day is spent bringing up children you may need to start the moment you are woken up. If it's weekends you lose track of, or the evening vanishes and you don't know what you've done, keep a time log – whenever it is you have the problem.

In the first column, marked Time, write down the time you start something and in the Activity column what you are doing. Then, every time you change activity note down the time and the new activity. You can either fill in the Time Spent column as you go along or update it a couple of times a day. What is important is that you fill in everything that you do – interruptions, changes of direction, 'wasting time', *everything*. Since you want a record of all the time you spend working don't forget to record time worked at home. If you read papers for a meeting over breakfast or if you catch up with paperwork in the evening, it should all go down. You want to find out exactly how many hours you work, and what you do with them.

Ideally, keep your time log for a week, but even a day is better than nothing. Or try a day – a different day – for several weeks. Some people find that the sheer discipline of having to write everything down alters what they do. Don't worry about this. You'll either quickly fall back into your old ways so that it won't matter, or you'll begin to sow seeds for new, useful habits, which is all to the good.

The Time Log on page 30 shows you what your completed time

Date:

Time	Activity	Time Spent

Time Log

log can look like. Invent your own shorthand and symbols to make keeping it easier. For example →phone means incoming calls, and phone→ means outgoing. Adding names helps even more when you look back to make sense of what you did. Note the time as you start or change tasks rather than doing this retrospectively.

When you've kept your time log you can then quickly add together all the time spent on the important activities you highlighted in Column 1 and fill in Column 3 on your Use of Time chart. Now compare Columns 1, 2 and 3. What does this tell you about your priorities? The use of your time? Also, look at the amount of time you spend in activities you consider peripheral, low priority or not your job. How much time do you spend thinking, planning, reviewing? How much time did you spend chatting, drinking coffee, daydreaming?

Some people will automatically say they can't keep a time log — they're on the move all the time or they're in a situation where recording changes would be inappropriate. Is this really true or do you simply mean you can't be bothered to do it? Are there ways round the problem? One man talked into a pocket Dictaphone all day (*Twin Peaks* style!) and his secretary transcribed it. This was, of course, additional work for her but in this case, since she was the one who insisted he attend a time management course, possibly she thought the investment of her time would have long-term benefits — for her. You can always record a block of time, if you're out of the office when you can't record fine detail, and then fill in as much as you can remember later. Not ideal, but certainly better than nothing.

For a couple of days write out a list of things you want to accomplish that day. At the end of the day compare your list with what you actually accomplished. If you didn't get everything done, why not? Where did you lose control of the day? Did you react to something that took you along a different track to the one you had intended to follow? Was it vital that you reacted then and there, or was it habit? Could you get back on track? Why didn't you?

Or maybe the problem was more to do with your list being totally unrealistic in the first place. Did you simply write down everything that needed to be done, rather than what you could hope to achieve

Date:

Time	Activity	Time Spent
8.50	Collect mail, chat to colleague	10
9.00	in office, listen to answerphone	6
9.06	mail	10
9.16	phone → AB	3
9.19	mail	2
9.21	→ phone AJ	2
9.23	mail	5
9.28	→ phone	2
9.30	read report	23
9.53	→ phone KM	3
9.56	leave for 10.00 examiners meeting	53
10.49	back in office, make coffee	2
10.51	meeting with statistician re research	39
11.30	mail	3
11.33	→ phone, Ph.D student	27
12.00	go for sandwiches	13
12.13	collect mail on way back	2
12.15	mail	5
12.20	coffee	3
12.23	eat sandwiches, mark essays	49

Time Log

in a day? Did you try to be realistic but underestimate how long everything takes?

One of the most common reactions people have to their time log is surprise at how little time they spend on any one activity in a block. My favourite story comes from a man who kept his log in the week after the New Year holiday. His longest piece of time on any activity was forty minutes — 'and that was when the Director came to wish me Happy New Year!' Research indicates that managers tend not to spend longer than ten minutes on any task before changing activities. This doesn't reflect how long tasks actually take, nor their importance, it is just a pattern of work. In fact, this is the pattern for most occupations, household chores included.

Another surprise is the amount of time that gets frittered away, not just on coffee and chatting but on trivial tasks. Allied to this is a new awareness of how long things really take and how inaccurate our estimates often are. In Chapter 4, when you really get to grips with planning your time, you'll need to be able to realistically estimate how long tasks take. This means you need to start considering now why you habitually underestimate the time needed.

Underestimating Time

Hidden Time Consumers

Often we look at the main part of a task and forget about all the little things that go on around it but which take time. This is particularly true if the task has an externally set time-limit. Suppose you are going to a meeting, or to give a presentation or a lecture, and you know that it is scheduled for one hour. Psychologically, and often literally, we set an hour aside for this and end up saying, 'I'm doing x between 10 and 11, that still gives me three hours this morning to get other things done.' Is this true? Leaving aside preparation time, where else does time go around this activity? This sequence of events is likely to be:

1 Find necessary papers:	anything from
– minutes/agendas/related reports	5 minutes
– notes/slides/charts	to hours
2 Flick through papers:	anything from
– to make sure it's all there	5 minutes
– to remind yourself what it is about	to hours
3 Prepare to leave:	
– loo, check hair/make-up/tie	couple of minutes
– coat on, papers into case etc.	1 minute
4 Tell secretary where you are going/leave instructions/switch 'phone through	couple of minutes
5 Leave	
6 (optional) Go back because you've forgotten something	
7 Travel to meeting	down corridor or across town
8 1 hour meeting	
9 Talk to people afterwards:	
– you're being sociable	couple of minutes
– people have questions	to hours
– want more information	
– raise related issues	
10 Travel back to your office	
11 'Debrief'	
– coat off	couple of minutes
– put papers away/drop on floor	to half an hour
– get a coffee 'because I deserve it after that'	
– chat over meeting with a colleague because it went well/badly/am I reading the signals right?/. . .	

Some of these activities may only take seconds, others considerable time depending on your personal organization (can you find the necessary papers?) or distance from the meeting. They are all legitimate (except, maybe, forgetting something), they all take time. What you have marked in your diary as 'one hour' really takes one hour fifteen minutes or even two hours, depending on how long you chat and so on. You don't have three hours of morning left, you have (considerably) less. When we're planning how much we can do in a day we tend to forget these hidden time consumers. And that's when we start to run behind schedule.

Trivial Pursuits

The reason we may forget the hidden time consumers above is because they're trivial and we assume that trivia doesn't, that is shouldn't, take up much time. But six one hour tasks in a day with ten minutes trivia attached to each of them adds on another hour.

There are all sorts of trivial tasks in a day, or tasks we see as not important, 'beneath us' or requiring little effort, and we therefore assume they take little or no time. Psychologically we see them as unimportant and therefore we either discount them or drastically underestimate the time they take. Look at your time log to identify both the tasks and the time involved.

'Time Flies When You're Having Fun'

It's true that we're much less likely to notice how long something takes if it's a task we enjoy; half an hour can seem like ten minutes, or you forget to stop for lunch when you're engrossed. We're also more likely to spin out tasks we like doing, or do them even if they are not really necessary, particularly when they are better than the next task.

You Don't Want To Do It

Things we don't want to do may make us spend longer on the previous task, but also underestimate the time it really takes because we can't face being realistic about something we don't like. This can be related to procrastination which we'll deal with in Chapter 7.

Perfectionism

High standards usually require more time – going over and over something, refining it, improving it, perfecting it all takes time. This might or might not be necessary, or even appropriate. This is another topic requiring more thought which we will return to in Chapter 7.

Maintenance Time Logs

If you're going through a period of getting to the end of the day or week and, whilst knowing that you've been working hard, wondering what you have to show for it, keep a maintenance time log to help you get back on track. Rather than record every changing activity, have a list of headings based on your most important areas of work (which you will sort out in Chapter 3). Under each note how much time (to the nearest five minutes) you spend on each. People who work on accounts/projects which get billed will be doing this anyway. You can then see where the problem is – where your time is going. If more time than you want is disappearing under one heading, you can start paying more attention to the tasks that you are recording here, and see what you are doing that is unnecessary or taking too long. If half your day finds its way under 'miscellaneous' then you need to find a few more headings, or recognize that this time is being spent on trivia.

⌛ PART 2

Where Are
You Going?

GOALS, DAYDREAMS AND CHORES

It is not enough to be busy.
The question is
What are you busy about?
HENRY DAVID THOREAU

I keep these words in the front of my diary as a timely reminder when I feel things getting out of control. You can work hard, but if you're working at the 'wrong' things you won't achieve your goal – whatever it is. Developing time management skills is less about doing things faster, or more efficiently, and more about working effectively – doing the 'right' things. In this chapter, we consider questions of where you're going and how you're going to get there. If you don't know where you're going, not only does it not matter which route you take but you won't even know when you've arrived.

We all have things we have to do, things we feel we should do, things we want to do, things we dream about doing. Our goals and priorities are set within our personal value system. I cannot tell you what your goals are, or even what they should be. Nor can I definitely tell you how you should achieve them. However, I can give you some guildelines.

Where Are You Going?

Our plans miscarry because they have no aim.
When a man does not know what harbour he is making for, no wind is the right wind.

SENECA

Now is the time to stop and consider who else is involved in your plans for the future. Before you can start listing your goals, what you want to do or achieve, take a few minutes out to focus on your life as a whole. At the end of the last chapter I gave you some very general questions to begin thinking about, to put you in the right frame of mind to begin developing goals and setting priorities.

You need to think about *all* the areas of your life and what you want to do in them if you are not to wake up one morning and realize that you are too old to win the US Open/be the youngest member of Parliament/have children/backpack around India/retire at 40/feel comfortable in a disco/start a new career in neurosurgery; or the children are leaving for college and the last time you really noticed them was when they set off for nursery school. Whether these disappointments have to do with biology, ability, attitudes or a combination doesn't matter, you suddenly feel 'past it': that something has passed you by. Even if you do decide to set off on the guru trail to India, it is not going to be the same at 40 or 50 as at 20.

Your life has a number of major areas (life areas) and you are likely to want to do things in all of them. A common mistake is for people to think time management has only to do with work, or that planning somehow spoils the spontaneity of personal life. I'm not suggesting that you set goals and plan every moment of your day, or life, but to think about how much you miss because you 'never get round to it'. Big things, like holidays, you, or someone else in the family, plan. But what about the weekend outing with the children/visits to the theatre/decorating the bedroom/learning a language/taking up jogging/needlepoint/the harmonica/tiddlywinks? How many times in the last month have you thought about doing something, or worse, promised someone you'd do something, and then let it go because 'something's come up at work'/'I've got to get this finished'/'I just didn't have time'?

Without thinking, we often set priorities we would question if we took the time to think. Usually it is our family life which suffers. The chart on page 39 lists the four major life areas: work, family, personal life and social life. Each of these will have sub-divisions and it is within these sub-divisions you will set goals. At the moment,

WORK

....
....
....
....
....
....

FAMILY

....
....
....
....

PERSONAL

....
....
....

SOCIAL

....
....
....

Major Life Areas

concentrate on just sorting out your major life areas rather than what you want to do. For most people, work (paid or unpaid) will take up the most space — both in terms of areas and time. List under each heading the areas in which you want to accomplish something.

Don't, at this point, get too detailed or you'll lose sight of the broad picture. You're aiming to get an overview of what is going on in your life as a whole, an overview that makes sure you don't lose touch with important areas through simple neglect. You need a list that you can see and take in easily.

Under work put down the areas that are part of your job, as well as additional things you have to take on and extra-mural but still work-related areas. Think in broad terms. Ask yourself what you are responsible for. What does your job description say?

Many people have a blind spot about certain aspects of their job, or have responsibilities which do not directly appear in their job description. One is people, another is communication. If you have anyone who works for you, in the sense that you exercise some authority over them, they report to you or you can give them tasks, then you are responsible for them and 'staff' should appear somewhere on your list. People running their own small business who do not employ a personnel manager (or someone with this as part of their job description) have this responsibility even if they often choose to overlook it until a problem arises or they need to hire staff. Anyone who has a secretary, even on a part-share, part-time basis, has some responsibility for, and to, him or her.

Communication is an another area people are often reluctant to acknowledge. Communicating verbally or in writing, formally or informally, is something we do more than we think. Other areas of responsibility which may or may not be obvious are: financial, administrative, long-term planning, major projects on a one-off basis, development and evaluation.

Any of these may have to be added to what you see as your 'real' job functions, whether this is patient care/making a sale/solving crimes/delivering a sermon/bringing up children/bringing in a project on budget and on time . . . A final area you may want to consider is best called 'professional updating'. Keeping up to date with new information, ideas, products and events is not something which happens by osmosis, neither should it be squeezed haphazardly into odd moments. If part of your job is to stay up to date (and this is generally an assumed job requirement rather than one which is spelt out) then you need to plan when this will happen. Students have often said to me (usually when they don't know something) '. . . but I've got the book'. Having the book is not the point: reading the book is only half the point, *thinking* about what you've read is the other part. *Implementing* what you've read, if appropriate, gets the bonus points.

It may take you several attempts to get your 'life areas' sorted out to your satisfaction. If you're running into trouble look at your time log, at all the tasks you have carried out, and ask yourself why you did them. If you can't come up with a good answer you're well on the way to realizing this isn't a task you should be doing at all.

The busier you are, the more you are involved in a number of different enterprises, the more important an overview is of what is going on in your life. True workaholics may be entirely focused on their work, but most of us believe there is more to life than just work. We are multifaceted people, wanting to do, or be, a number of different things. We all fulfil a number of different roles. Although this can present problems in the form of contradictory goals, wanting to be in two places at once, or do more than one thing at a time, the positive aspects of a full and interesting life outweigh the hassles. And part of this lies in not forgetting what it was that you wanted to do.

Whether you're writing down life areas or goals (which we're coming to) these aren't 'tablets of stone'. You can always change your mind and decide something isn't important after all. What does matter is that this happens as a result of conscious thought, choice and decision-making – rather than by default.

Goals

Under each of your life areas you can now start to develop your goals: everything from 'I want a change of career' to 'I want to be closer to my family'. They can be long-term or short-term, major achievements or minor successes, it doesn't matter at the moment. There are a number of 'rules' when setting goals which help in planning.

Be Positive

In as far as it is possible, set your goals in positive terms: *not* 'I'm going to stop taking on so much'; *but* 'I'm only going to agree to do things I know I have time to do and which fit my priorities'.

Be Specific

It's easy to get lost in a morass of vague, ill-defined goals. Being specific is about defining what you mean. All too often people set goals as a nebulous state to be achieved, usually along the lines of being 'better' in some way, without thinking through what they mean. Your goal might be 'to be rich', 'to be successful'. You need to spell out what this means, for you. Does being 'rich' mean having £1,000,000 in the bank or not being in the red? Does being 'successful' mean being a director of ICI or getting a job? wearing designer clothes or the freedom to wear what you like? Even if your goal in reading this book started out as 'to have more time', did you have an idea of whether you were looking for an extra hour a day, an extra few weeks somewhere or for time to slow down to half pace while you keep your own speed going?

Make Your Goal Measurable

This ties in with being specific. It always helps to know when you've reached your goal, so it needs to be measurable. Most of us would choose to be happy rather than unhappy, but is this something you can aim for without understanding what 'being happy' means to you, and some way of knowing when you are? Is being happy a stable state you can reach and stay in? Is it not something which comes and goes? The most measurable you might get here is to say that you want to feel happy more often than you don't. Even then to achieve this goal you need to know what to do to encourage yourself to feel happy. Some concepts or goals may be difficult to measure, but some sort of standard is necessary if you are not to continually chase a goal that forever moves out of your reach. You can always revise your standards, and by doing so you have the opportunity to reflect on what you have done so far, and whether continuing on this same path is the option you really want.

Make it Achievable

Achievable, or some might say, realistic. This is the 'rule' that is most often contentious. The argument against goals being achievable or realistic is that it puts a limit on a person's aspirations, that no one knows what they are capable of until they've tried, that it is only by reaching for the impossible that we discover new things and so on. The argument from the other side is that unrealistic goals become demoralizing if you don't achieve them and that they can stop you doing or enjoying the things you can do. They give people false expectations.

Both sides of the argument are true in part. It depends on your personality, and to some extent your culture, which you opt for.

Some people see the attainment of a goal very much as a series of steps up a ladder and they set their sights firmly on the next rung, or possibly one beyond. This is something they can do and be almost certain of achievement. They may well understand that having achieved that goal they will immediately go on to set another goal.

Other people prefer to set their sights high – 'go for gold' is their motto. If they are sensible they know that to reach this apparently unattainable goal they have to progress through a number of subsidiary stages, but they have their sights firmly fixed on the top.

As cultures, Britain tends to favour the former and the USA the latter. Both have their advantages and disadvantages. If you choose the 'go for gold' approach you do need some realistic assessment of your chances of reaching it, and if you don't get there, recognize these odds, along with how far you have travelled. Rather than looking at the successes they have, some people only look at how far they have to go, or see not getting the gold as evidence of failure. This can be demoralizing and damaging to both self-esteem and motivation. If you tend to think like this then you will be better served by having attainable goals.

Another advantage of not being totally fixed on one 'big', out-of-reach goal, is that it is often easier to see alternative routes, follow interesting options, challenges and sidelines as they occur, possibly changing direction altogether if you are frequently resetting, and thus revising, your goals. Of course, the person with narrow sights and a fixed goal will see this as a disadvantage.

Time Bounded

Goals have to have a deadline, or at least a date by which you will have started something and made a move towards obtaining what you want. For something to be truly a goal you need to be doing something towards achieving it – if not today, then at least this week. Or, if it is postponed, you need a good reason why, and a clear indication of when you are going to make a start. Goals without deadlines often become daydreams (see page 50).

Worthwhile

Your goals must be important to you. There is no point in other people telling you to try for something if it doesn't interest you. Motivation is one of the keys to change. No one can change for you, and it is very much harder to change to please someone other than yourself. People sent on time management courses by harried secretaries, fraught assistants or distraught partners rarely change – unless the person sending them can wield a big enough stick to 'motivate' them: 'I never see you anymore. There's no point in being married to you. I want a divorce' is one; 'I can't stand your disorganization any longer. I'm applying for a transfer' is another. But in either case the person whose behaviour has to change will find it difficult to maintain it unless they too get something out of it. Reasons why change can be so difficult will be explored more fully in Chapters 7 and 8.

Feedback

Some checking system needs to be incorporated so that you can assess whether you have met your goals and then whether this has bought the rewards you hoped for. If something went wrong, why? What have you learnt? If something went right, it is equally important to ask why, so that you can repeat the elements of success in the future. This might even require a planning system which reminds you at some time in the future to check back on goals attained. With hindsight, were you successful? Was it what you wanted? What were the long-term consequences?

Change and development

Although not quite of 'rule' status, making goals capable of change and development is sensible. If you are following an 'achievable' plan this will happen anyway. Periodically it is useful to reassess your goals in view of changes in your life, external changes in your job or company, and in terms of the world around you.

One trap to avoid falling into is focusing all your attention on one goal with nothing to replace it. This is especially true if, although reaching it may be personally satisfying, the goal doesn't make any immediate or real difference to your life.

One example of this I frequently come across is students obtaining their Ph.D. For a minimum of three years everything they have been doing at work has been focused towards this end. They get it, there is a sudden heady thrill of being called 'Dr' for the first time and then, often, a feeling of let down, a sense of 'is that it?' This is particularly true if the student is already in another job – getting the Ph.D. doesn't always mean promotion, or more money, or anything else tangible. It is an academic hurdle successfully negotiated. It is also

Sub-area: CREATION

Major Task 1. Create 'New World' (Heaven and Earth)		
Steps	Deadline Time starts ... now!	Feedback 'Is It Good?'
i Need light – day and night	Day One	
ii Create sky (heaven) – (above and below!)	Day Two	
iii Create dry land – (divide earth and seas)	Day Three	
iv Create plants (grass, herbs, trees etc.)		
v Arrange for lights in sky – (two main lights? Sun and moon?)	Day Four	
vi Organize time – days, years and so on		
vii Populate sea and air	Day Five	need for replacements?
viii Creatures for land – cattle, beasts, 'creeping things'	Day Six	find better name for last lot!
ix Create Man in my own image		(is this really a good idea?) needs instructions 'be fruitful and multiply'
x REST	Day Seven	Project needs checking up on in future – possibly a job for son?

Life Area 1: Work

the last academic hurdle. Suddenly all that is ahead is flat track. In such cases, the now ex-students report that they go into a 'low' for two or three weeks and then slowly begin to appreciate their success and enjoy it. Other goals are usually appearing by then.

If you only have one goal, no matter how big or how important, when you have achieved it you are more likely to feel cast adrift than euphoric. A number of overlapping goals, with variable time scales, is more likely to enable you to weather success, to really enjoy what you achieve without feeling that all purpose, everything that has motivated you, has gone.

Models of good time management and goal setting are around us all the time, we just need to pay attention and learn from them. Consider, for a moment, that within your job description 'creation' is a task. What might your goals be? How might you set out a plan? Would it look like the one on page 46?

This plan emphasizes the step by step goal approach, building in deadlines, feedback, and, most important of all, time for rest. We will come back to issues of planning in the next chapter. For now we will return to a few more things to do with goal setting.

Goals at Work

Work is the refuge of people who have nothing better to do.
OSCAR WILDE

You need to consider how far your goals at work fit in with your company's goals — or even your boss's goals. Goals at work can be divided into two areas: what I will call work-work goals, and personal-work goals.

Work-work goals are things to be done or achieved which fall directly within the remit of your job description. They are the things you are paid to do. A problem arises if you equate having goals only with having ambition. Ambition can be driven by many things, including fear. Goals can be steps to fulfilling ambitions, but they can also be fairly mundane things which simply have to be done. Getting your report finished/your department budget finalized/your filing up to date/the exam papers marked/the ironing done before the family run out of clean clothes . . . are all goals. They are not necessarily the strivings of ambition.

Personal-goals are more likely to be fuelled by ambition. These are the things which may be only tangential to your job, but which will get you noticed. Or goals involving learning new skills so you will be able to be promoted. They may be more mundane goals which will make your working life simpler, more streamlined and efficient, but which are neither high profile nor really part of your job description.

When planning your working day (or week), as we will in the next chapter, a balance has to be kept between work-work goals and personal-work goals. Many people who complain of 'too much to do' or who have problems with priorities have fallen into the trap of believing that personal-work goals carry the same weight as work-work goals. Of course to you they will, indeed personal-work goals will probably be the most important and the most exciting. But as far as the company is concerned, it is the work-work goals they are paying you for and want to see achieved. Making the mistake of assuming that you can devote equal amounts of time to both, in working hours, is one of the easiest ways to become frustrated and feel that you have poor time management.

Using the layout on page 49, I suggest you write out what you believe the goals of the organization or company you work for are, and then your department's goals. Go back and look at your work goals. How do they relate to the company? If they don't, does it matter? What are you going to do about it? At the end of the day profit is the goal of most business, and even if you work in the public sector, in the health service or public education, someone, somewhere believes the objective is to come in on budget and not overspend, rather than save lives or educate children. If you find you don't agree with all your company's goals, how are you going to live with that?

One school of management believes that everybody should know what the company's goals are and should be focused on the end

COMPANY'S GOALS

....
....
....
....
....
....

DEPARTMENT'S GOALS

....
....
....
....
....
....

product (if not the profits), and that they should know their place in the grand scheme of things. It is believed that this produces more motivated and committed employees. It certainly doesn't do any harm to remember what you are about globally, and this helps you to see where your priorities lie.

There is a well-known story that reminds us of this. Two medieval stonemasons were asked what they were doing. The first said he was shaping stones into rectangular blocks, the second said he was building a cathedral.

There are no prizes for guessing who is likely to be the more motivated, better able to set priorities and shake off the boredom and frustration that inevitably occurs sometimes. What is your cathedral?

Before we can move on to think about setting priorities, a little more needs to be said about two problems in goal setting: daydreams and chores.

Daydreams

Daydreams are simply that: the things we dream about doing – fantasies of what we might achieve or become. There is nothing wrong with them, in fact they can serve useful functions, rewarding and encouraging us, replacing painful thoughts, relieving stress and frustration while waiting in a traffic jam . . . and so on. Daydreams only become a problem when we pretend they are goals. If you really wanted to you could make a distinction between daydreams and fantasies. Fantasies are things which will *never* happen, daydreams *could*, but are unlikely to.

For 99.99 per cent of people reading this book winning Wimbledon (even playing at Wimbledon) is a fantasy. Improving your tennis is a goal. Learning a foreign language could be a goal, but for most people it is a daydream. It is something they *say* they want to do – 'If only I had more time' – but never get around to doing. In their mind, it is a goal, by their behaviour it is a daydream. Such daydream goals are remarkably similar for most of us. They tend to be learning a foreign language, mastering a musical instrument or some other artistic skill, or travel. This reflects our general neglect of the creative or adventurous parts of our selves. They are also things we often wish we had learnt as children.

Too many daydreams masquerading as goals can increase stress and frustration. You either have to really make it a goal, fit it into your schedule and set time limits, or give it up to the realm of daydreams. No one ever accepts how long it takes to learn something as an adult. We expect instant success – Chopin before we've mastered Chopsticks. If it's a priority, find time for it, otherwise let it go. That doesn't mean it has gone for good, you can always revive it later, if your situation or priorities change, but it does mean you don't have to worry about not doing anything now. Do you have a 'goal' you haven't done anything about for a couple of weeks? a few months? a year? Maybe you should recognize that it's not a goal, it's a daydream.

Chores

Every job has its chores. I've yet to meet anyone who doesn't think that some part of their job (paid and unpaid) shouldn't be done by them, usually because it's defined as 'menial' or below them in some way. At home we define much of the maintenance of our lives and home environment as chores. We either get on and do them, pay someone else to do them for us, or delegate them (to our partner, a member of our family or to our children). (*Note*: Delegation is not about offloading things you don't want to do, at least at work it's not, and we will explore it more thoroughly in Chapter 10.)

It might be quite true that someone paid less than you could do the chore equally well, but if it's part of your job, or there isn't anyone else to do it, then accept it. It might not be the greatest use of your time to spend ten minutes at the photocopier, but what are the alternatives? If there are none, then do it without a fuss, and in the least disruptive way as possible. We'll explore how in the next chapter.

Many things that people define as chores – because they're not very exciting – really come under the heading of work-work goals.

If you're having any difficulty establishing goals, or are overwhelmed by their number, try the exercise on page 52. Write down up to twenty different adjectives to describe yourself in work situations in Column 1. Cover this list, and in Column 2 write down up to twenty adjectives to describe yourself in relationships with your family and friends. Again, cover the list and in Column 3 write down adjectives to describe how you see yourself in personal activities or in a personal sense. In the last column, write down adjectives you would ideally like to use to describe yourself.

Another version of this would be to write down how you see yourself and how you think others (family, friends, colleagues, boss, subordinates, peers) see you.

However you do this, divide the lists of adjectives in Columns 1, 2 and 3 into three categories, positive, negative and neutral. How do the lists compare with your ideal list? What are your strengths and weaknesses? Do the lists overlap or are they quite different? Are there gaps? Are there words on your ideal list that don't appear anywhere

	work	relationships	personal	ideal
1				
2				
3				
4				
5				
6				
7				
8				
9				
10				
11				
12				
13				
14				
15				
16				
17				
18				
19				
20				

else? Are there worrying differences between how you see yourself
and how others see you? What are you going to do about it? This
exercise can help you put goals into perspective as you start seeing
them in relation to yourself.

Priorities

By now you might be beginning to feel overwhelmed by your lists
of goals and things to do. How does this help you to manage your
time? You might even feel worse than when you started, now that
you see laid out before you exactly what it is that needs doing. The
quotation by Thoreau at the start of the chapter should be your
answer — you have to do the 'right' thing. The nineteenth-century
Italian economist Vilfredo Pareto described what has become known
as the 80/20 rule. He pointed out that 20 per cent of Italian people
owned 80 per cent of the wealth. This is frequently restated as 20
per cent of what you do yields 80 per cent of the results. You may
see this in terms of 20 per cent of customers accounting for 80 per
cent of sales, or 20 per cent of the staff/students/patients/parish-
ioners/customers . . . causing 80 per cent of the trouble.

One of the secrets of successful time management is to know which
20 per cent of your activity produces 80 per cent of the results! This
includes assessing where your greatest pay-offs lie, what gives you
greatest satisfaction, what serves your goals most. Some of the other
80 per cent can be dispensed with, but not all. Some of this time
will be spent on chores that are probably boring but ultimately
necessary.

In the same way that you have to work out your goals for yourself,
ultimately you also have to work out your own priorities. I could say
that the 'major' parts of your job are your priorities, or that what helps
you achieve your main goals are priorities, but does this really help?

If you've been asked to work late and your child has a starring role
in the school play, what are you going to do? Or, you're cancelling
an outing with your partner for the fourth time in as many weeks
to work overtime? Or, you've a report to get out by the end of the

day and your boss asks you to get something else done as a priority, as well? Or, you're invited to become involved in a new, exciting and potentially time-consuming project when you're only just keeping your head above water?

One thing to realize is that there is no one right answer. Ultimately your priorities are set by your value system. Sometimes your family will, should, indeed must come first. At other times it will be your job. Sometimes you can pass the decision back to your boss — which of the two high priority, urgent tasks is the least urgent? Sometimes, the opportunity is too great to miss and worth extra, short-term, effort.

Your priorities are not always what you think they are at first sight. A group of people who all run their own small businesses started by saying their priorities were 'to make money' and 'to be successful/ rich'. On further investigation we found that a number of them could earn more or at least the same amount for less hours by working for someone else. It turned out their real priority was 'to be independent', 'to have autonomy' and 'to be responsible to myself'. Despite long hours and a sometimes uncertain future, for each of these men the freedom of having their own business was their highest priority and thus their greatest motivation.

Whatever you say, your behaviour describes your priorities. If you forget someone's birthday/don't visit a friend/don't write to a relative ... what you are saying is that it wasn't important enough to you.

Deciding on priorities means distinguishing between what is urgent, but trivial, and what is non-urgent but important. It means asking 'What am I prepared to give up so that I can take this on?' It requires decisions about how often you can let someone down and still have them trust you. Past experience and future expectations are important. Watching your child's first stage performance may be more important than his or her tenth.

There are no foolproof tricks to setting priorities. Sometimes it's easy, sometimes it isn't. To take some of the pain out of the decision-making process there are a few exercises you can do:

1. If you have a list of tasks and don't know where to start divide the tasks into three categories:

A   Must do
B   Should do
C   Nice-to-do or Would-like-to-do

Work-work goals usually fit into 'must do' with a few into 'should do', but personal-work goals are harder to classify. You want to change jobs, which means learning a new skill. It's a 'must do' but it can't take priority over other 'must do' work goals. *A*s get done before *B*s which get done before *C*s.

2.   If you are still thinking about goals in general and don't know where to start, go back to the major life areas and goals described on page 39, and using the chart on page 56 list up to ten goals in each area. Now give each goal a score from 4 (couldn't be more important) to 1 (little importance/it can wait).

    Now on the next chart on page 57, relist your goals so that all the 4s are together, all the 3s, and so on. This gives you an overview of what is important in your life and helps you judge family goals against work, personal against social and so on.

3.   If your list of goals has priorities set against them such as 'urgent', 'very urgent', 'urgentish' or 'top priority', you need to develop a effective triage system. If the A–B–C system above isn't working for you, you need to question where it is breaking down and why. Is it that you can't distinguish what is important to you from more global needs? Go back to your list and look at two things: (i) Outcome; (ii) Likelihood of Success. This allows you to take account of changing external conditions.

    Doctors freely talk of triage – who gets treated first. Usually, it is the most seriously ill/injured. After a disaster an accident and emergency department will be overwhelmed but staff can be pulled in from departments elsewhere, off-duty staff come in and patients can be transferred to other hospitals if necessary. Medics operating in a war zone, however, have to make the same decisions but with different external circumstances. There are no more staff, no more hospitals. There may have to be a decision not to treat the most seriously injured with little chance of survival in order to save the seriously injured with a better chance

	work	family	personal	social
1				
2				
3				
4				
5				
6				
7				
8				
9				
10				

Goals

4	3	2	1

Goals

of survival (and whose survival chances will decrease if they are left). Be thankful that no matter how difficult your decisions they aren't as difficult as this.

To make sense of triage you need information on:

• The best chance of success
• The impact of chance of success on other people
• The outcome measures

To move forward in priority setting you must ask questions about what you do. You may have already been doing this but in a simplistic way – 'If I do x then I'll get y'. To be really useful your questions need to be more detailed: think about what will happen not only if you say 'yes' to something, but also if you say 'no'.

Saying Yes and Saying No

• What will you achieve by doing x? What kind of major and minor gains does x bring? Short-term? Long-term?
• What will happen (realistically) if you don't do x? How much does this matter? Short-term? Long-term?
• What are your chances of doing x and succeeding? Failing?
• What will you learn from doing (or trying) x, whether you succeed or fail?
• What is the best that could happen if you do x? How likely is this? Can you accept these odds?
• Is the effort involved in doing x worth the gains?
• What is the worst that could happen to you if you don't do x? Try and fail? Can you cope with the consequences?
• Are there alternatives to x?
• Are there things you can do to make success more likely? Make the effort less? Is it worth it?
• Are there things you can give up to make taking on x more possible?
• What will happen if you don't make a decision? Is this the same as trying and not succeeding? Which is better?

When people are faced with alternative choices the difficulty encountered in making the decision varies with the type of choice to be made. If you are asked to choose between two things you want to do, most people make this choice fairly easily. One option almost always has an edge. Making a decision between two things you don't want to do is also fairly easy – especially if you opt, as most people do, for neither and go off and do something entirely different. The difficult decision is when your choice is one of both attraction and avoidance. There are pluses and minuses. Weighing these sensibly will help you make the best decision. If necessary, using the above questions, write out a list of pros and cons.

In general terms men seem better at planning their careers than women, mainly because they are encouraged to do this from an early age. Women, however, may need to set priorities and plan their careers more carefully than men if they intend to have children. There is no rule about when it is best to have children. Taking time out when you are established can be just as much of a problem as when you are starting. Children do not necessarily get easier as they get older. A 10-year-old is less likely to want a childminder than a 2-year-old – but needs one just as much. I have met women who planned to have (and succeeded) their children at 'quiet times' in their work year (teachers and academics chose the summer, for example), but this requires co-operative biological processes that no one can guarantee.

Priorities in Perspective

Like everything else, priorities are not, and need not, be immutable. They can and will change. There are times in a person's working life when their career will be most important, at other times relationships, family and children will take precedence. When you're building a career, it is common to let personal interests slip away beneath a mountain of work and possible achievements. This need not be permanent unless you choose to make it so. For some people, career as top priority is more a sign of lack of confidence in their ability or fear than it is ambition. Sometimes time is the only answer to this, as you consolidate your position you feel more secure. Or an honest, realistic appraisal of your vulnerability may tell you things aren't as bad as your habitually gloomy prognostications.

Priorities can be long-term and many of us have a tendency to think only in terms of the distant future. But what of short-term priorities? Big decisions are often easier to make than little ones. You are more likely to sit down and sensibly evaluate the pros and cons, probably discussing the matter with colleagues, friends and family, so that you play out different scenarios as you talk things over. Those frustrating little decisions are likely to be the greatest cause of stress to the poor time manager.

At such times, working something out is as much about getting your anxieties into perspective as sorting out your priorities. You can't do it all, no matter what you may want to believe. It is helpful to have a formula question to ask yourself at such times, to gain distance and perspective: this should not be 'If the house were on fire would I save my work or the kids?' (note *my* work, but *the* kids – if this is what you say what does this tell you about values and priorities?), or 'If my partner was in an accident would I rush off to the hospital or finish this report?' These are, I hope, things which you wouldn't have to think about (which reflects my value system). Something more lighthearted is called for to ease the tension and assist perspective.

Asking the question 'Will it matter in five years whether I've done this?' or 'Will it matter next week whether this is finished now or tomorrow morning?' helps. Both these allow for a 'yes' answer, but whether you say yes or no you've gained perspective for your decision-making. To really put something in perspective, however, I think something even more frivolous is called for. You need to use your own daydreams (or maybe that should be fantasy) to bring your minor anxieties into perspective – when you're fretting about what you should be doing, when you have to work tonight even though you're shattered, or you can't go out as planned because you have to finish x. Mine is: if Clint Eastwood arrived at my door tonight and asked me out to dinner would I go or would I say 'Sorry Clint, I have to get this chapter finished'? So far, Clint has won every time!

FROM HERE TO ... NEXT WEEK

To everything there is a season, and a time for every purpose under heaven:

A time to be born, and a time to die: a time to plant, and a time to pluck up that which is planted;

A time to kill, and a time to heal; a time to break down, and a time to build up:

A time to weep, and a time to laugh; a time to mourn, and a time to dance;

A time to cast away stones, and a time to gather stones together; a time to embrace, and a time to refrain from embracing;

A time to get, and a time to lose; a time to keep, and a time to cast away;

A time to rend, and a time to sew; a time to keep silence, and a time to speak;

A time to love, and a time to hate; a time of war, and a time of peace.

ECCLESIASTES 3.1–9

When planning for the future, whether next year or this afternoon, we need to consider, in as far as we can, everything that will happen. This includes the bad as well as the good. Very often, the bad is unexpected and can't be planned for, but it will inevitably happen sometimes. The passage from Ecclesiastes reminds us that there is a time to get, but there is also a time to lose. If you want to believe that time management, or planning, means you will never lose, that you will always have time for everything you want to do, you are going to be disappointed. No one can give you that. No one can have that. What we are concerned about in this chapter is maximizing the possibility of achieving your goals, your priorities, not guaranteeing them. To start this, you need to ask, what can I do today to make the future happen? To bring my goals nearer?

Planning

There are no acceptable excuses for not planning. The most common given is 'I have so much to do I don't have time to plan/organize my life'. Look at what you're doing and ask yourself whether an hour a week would make a difference to your workload. The chances are that it won't — so take an hour a week to start planning, start organizing. Losing an hour is unlikely to increase substantially the mess you're in, but it will go a long way to helping you find a way out.

Look at your work habits, and your time log, to see how often time is wasted because of poor planning. How often have you rushed into action because a deadline seemed near, only to have to do something again because, without all the details, it wasn't done appropriately the first time? Or, you've rushed ahead with something in the hope of making an early start, only to come to an abrupt halt because colleagues haven't done their bit, or a delivery hasn't arrived, because none of your plans coincided.

The biggest misconception people have about planning is that it inevitably adds time to a project. The case is quite the reverse — it shortens the total completion time because every aspect is co-ordinated and nothing is forgotten. Bear in mind the comment, 'There's never time to do it properly, but there's always time to do it again!' Think back to the last time you had to do something again because of mistakes. What would have taken least time: to plan it, do it and have it go right, or to rush in, do it, have it go wrong, then go back and do it again? Which method gives you greatest satisfaction? Which scenario makes you look most competent?

Maybe the reason you don't like planning is more psychological. You don't like the idea of being organized because you value spontaneity. To you, planning is the equivalent of a ritual of boredom. All well and good if you have enough time in which to be spontaneous, but if you haven't . . .

Or is your problem that you're a doer rather than a thinker? Do you identify with the sentiment, 'Let's get the show on the road?' In your case, planning is likely to make you feel uneasy because it requires thought rather than action, sitting still rather than rushing about. There is, apparently, little to show for the time spent. If you are someone who likes, or needs, to see quick results then planning with lists and charts gives you a visible result of your deliberations, both for yourself and other people to see where your time went.

Planning should never be used as an excuse to avoid action. You are unlikely ever to develop the perfect, foolproof plan, but you should aim to bring some order to the otherwise chaos of your goals and tasks. Planning, order, regularity in habits, actions, and tasks can become a way of life and be recognized by others as such. In the 1720s John Wesley became a member of a religious group at Oxford University that, characterized by the order and regularity with which they approached their studies and religious observances, became known as 'Methodists'.

The first step in planning is to move from goals to tasks.

From Goals to Tasks

The longest journey must begin with the first step.
CONFUCIUS

What many people find daunting is the size of the goal and the length of time it will take to get there: 'It's not worth starting this now because I don't have time to finish it'; 'I'll do it when I've got this out the way and the decks are clear'; and 'It'll take two weeks and I don't have two weeks'. No one ever has two weeks. Looking for big pieces of time is an excuse, and so is waiting for the load to lighten a bit – unless past experience has taught you that some months are genuinely less busy than others. The only way to tackle major goals or big projects is to use the well-known S-method. S for salami:

Q: How do you eat a whole salami?
A: A slice at a time.

If it helps, and this depends on your culinary inclinations, envisage your big projects as major (as in army) or mammoth (as in woolly) tasks which you eat mouthful by mouthful (thus becoming the M-method).

Whichever way you chose to think of your goal you need to break it down into smaller tasks — manageable steps. It would be an unusual person indeed who didn't do this naturally much of the time. When it works we don't think about it. When it doesn't . . . well, there could be many reasons. The first and simplest solution is to review the steps needed to achieve the goal. How much you break goals down into tasks or steps depends on the type of task, your personality, your memory, and how much else is going on in your life. If you like making lists you will naturally gravitate to longer lists with smaller tasks. There is nothing wrong with this unless you have a tendency towards the obsessional, in which case limit your list-making, don't go for the smallest possible step and don't keep rewriting it. It's very easy to get carried away, with your major goals sub-divided into major tasks, divided again into minor tasks which are further divided and broken down.

Develop a system which suits you — the simplest system which is useful, doesn't allow you to forget anything, doesn't take too long to develop and maintain, and isn't so complicated that you forget what it means/can't decide where to write something/find it more effort than it's worth. The minute you get to your fourth sub-heading you're in trouble.

You're building a set of steps to lead you to what you want, they are not a barrier to achievement. And we all know that steps come in many shapes and forms: there are the long, shallow steps of the flyover crossing the busy road over which it's easy to push a baby buggy, or there are the steep steps of the Pyramids, when you need someone to help you up. Make your steps appropriate to you, the task, and the situation.

When writing your list of tasks or the steps to achieve a goal, remember to write in dates — usually the date by which something has to be completed, but sometimes the date you start (a diet or giving up cigarettes). If the tasks are not going to be completed by you alone,

1   Venue/date
2   Speakers
3   Publicity
4   Catering
5   Sponsorship
6   Publication
7   Travel arrangement
8   Social activities
9   . . .

3 PUBLICITY: tasks

	by	who	done
1 get advertising leaflet designed	Dec	LA	
2 get costing for journal advertisements	Dec	AC	
3 send adverts to journals	Jan-March		
4 leaflets printed			
5 list (with addresses) relevant individuals/institutions to send to	Dec	AC/all	
6 send out flyers	Jan		
7 design application form	Dec	LA	

Conference: Major Areas

and in many big projects they won't be, also note who is responsible for each task. The chart above begins to list the major areas involved in organizing a conference, and then sub-divides the tasks. The more complicated the project or task you're working on, the more important it is to you, or the more it costs you, the more detailed your lists are likely to be if you're not to forget anything. Who has tried to organize a big wedding without hundreds of lists? Or a new factory development? Or moving house? Or the annual conference?

Note that by having a date by which things have to be done you can add to your list as you think of things. It is *not* chronological, and therefore does *not* require rewriting (obsessionally neat people please note!). Either have a column to tick things off in as you do them, or cross them through, or both, whichever gives you greater satisfaction.

For things that have to be done, but which you don't like doing, or don't want to do, some people find it helps to break the task down into very small steps, so that even half an hour's work means you can cross something off. Others find the sight of a long list even more depressing and daunting. It depends on personality and mood. One woman reported that when renovating her house she started off by thinking in terms of rooms — 'We'll get the kitchen done first, then the living room' — but after several years of hard work, much expense and still more than half the house to do, she had a list for each room as she came to it, broken down into tiny steps so that an evening with the sander or a paintbrush meant something could be crossed off the list. It was important to her to keep in front of her what she was achieving rather than how far they still had to go. A long series of tasks in this case wasn't off-putting.

Some people, when writing out a series of steps towards a goal, include something they can cross off the minute the list is finished. This instant reward motivates them to get on with the next thing.

If steps are too big it can seem pointless writing them down — you know you won't forget and it doesn't help you plan as there is not enough detail about what has to be done. In writing this book I could have had two big steps:

1. Find a publisher
2. Write book

This isn't of any help. What I did have was a chart to fill in, once I'd got an agreement with the publisher, about what had to be done by when, how many chapters had to be written a month. Because I knew chapters would get altered and revised I had extra columns to accommodate this. Design your own charts/lists/steps to suit your own purpose and don't be limited by what is commercially available if nothing seems right. How you keep all this together we'll discuss shortly.

This Year, Next Year, Sometime, Never

You should now be in a position to be able to say with a modest degree of certainty what your goals are and the steps needed to get there. Although people often speak of goals in terms of a number of years — most frequently five — question how far ahead you can reasonably plan. The further it is, the more uncertain you will be and the less you can control.

New medical students know it will take five years to get their degrees but they need not start planning yet for the specialty they hope to enter. In part they do not have enough information or experience to really know what they are going to be best at and enjoy most, and external circumstances may change. Most medical students will become general practitioners, because that is where the need is and how the system works. Only a minority enter medical school planning to do this. They are more likely to have the glint of surgical steel in their eye as they dream of becoming a consultant surgeon. But whatever their long-term goals for their career development, for most of them long-term goals focus on getting through each year's exams.

For the most part, goals will fall into three categories:

Long-term: 1 year+
Medium-term: months
Short-term: weeks/days

By developing your goals into a series of steps it becomes much easier to determine exactly what it is you have to do today to achieve your goal next year.

A final word on steps and setting dates. For goals which have a fixed, unchangeable deadline you should always begin your planning backwards from that date. Although you might discover that you should have started months ago, at least you can spread the extra work evenly, rather than optimistically cramming more and more in your plan as the deadline approaches. And any set of plans should have some slippage built into it, based on past experience of what is appropriate. Never assume that everything will go without a hitch this time. At some point Murphy's Law or one of its variants will come into play. In a perfect world this wouldn't happen. How close is your world to perfection? We could look back at the 'Creation' plan on page 46 and wonder whether some of the days couldn't have been evened out a bit more, and whether some of the world's current problems aren't due to a rushed job to get finished. The creation of Man was a task crammed in at the end of a busy week. Maybe God was tired. But then we don't know what other work was on in the early days, do we? Note also the importance of rest. There was no running over into a day off to finish the job.

Developing a System

Before we go any further you need to develop a physical system by which you keep track of the pieces of paper you're generating from your various sets of lists. The 1980s saw the rise of the Filofax. Filofax, although a brand name, has become in most people's minds a generic term for a personal organizer. Your 'system' can be as elaborate or as simple as you like. There are a number of organizer systems on the market enabling you to carry everything around with you. You could try a system provided for you by one of the time management companies, but remember, they have a vested interest in getting you hooked on using as many different kinds of paper as possible, as well as having everything written out in detail since, at the end of the day, paper products are what they sell.

I prefer to take the '*Blue Peter* approach' – a children's television programme specializing in projects (you know: 'with the insides of two toilet rolls, an empty Cornflakes box, a large ball of string and a dog round your feet, you too can make a nuclear warhead – and here's one I made earlier'!) and encourage you to devise your own system, bearing in mind a few general rules. Something you have developed will end up serving you better than trying to reorganize what you do into someone else's system. By all means buy an organizer cover and spend time looking at all the available page designs so you can choose what suits you best. If you do get seduced by the variety and you start with too much you will feel obliged to use it and try to work it into your system.

You don't have to have an organizer if you prefer a conventional diary, but I suggest a looseleaf system of some kind is best for your planner and information system. The advantages of a looseleaf system is once something is written out you don't have to rewrite it in next year's diary, or carry the two diaries together. It is easy to add and discard things/pages as required and you don't end up with lots of loose scraps tucked in a diary or notebook which invariably get lost, or fall out. And if you have any obsessional traits it gives you virtually unlimited opportunities to play with coloured paper, sections, tabs, labels, charts and so on (a tendency which needs to be firmly kept in check).

Even with a personal organizer you don't need to keep *everything* in it. I think it is unnecessary to walk around all day with all the information on your life areas tucked under your arm. Since one criticism of organizers is that they are too big, cutting out some of this and maintaining it in one loose leaf file (possibly at home) seems reasonable. Now organizers have become passé and are no longer the fashionable symbols of the yuppie, you may feel more inclined to overcome your prejudice against them and evaluate their usefulness. Price, size and aesthetics all need to be considered when making your choice.

If you're worried about losing your organizer and watching your life disintegrate without it, don't be. Just as it is very rare for a woman who habitually carries a handbag to lose it, you are unlikely simply to put it down and forget it. They are rarely stolen — it is almost always because someone has left it in a car and the car is stolen. If it makes you feel more secure put a note in the front to the effect that you will pay a reward for its return in the event of it going missing.

However you organize your system, three parts are basic.

Planner

This is your overview, the information that is your decision-making base. It contains your life areas, and sections on goals broken down into tasks and steps. You do not necessarily need to carry all this around with you. A looseleaf system lets you take out relevant sections, for meetings and so on, and thus allows you to carry a much smaller system on a daily basis. The decision is yours. Whatever you do, remember its main purpose is to provide you with all the information you need about your life and aspirations to make decisions and set priorities. It functions as your memory, and also as a measure of commitment. Something written down is often more powerful than something you've merely thought.

'Don't forget' lists belong here, instead of on scraps of paper. One list covers small, one-off tasks – tasks which are finished in a short time, don't belong under other sections, require little following up and where timing is not particularly important; things which never make it into the formal goals section.

Diary

Again, it is your choice whether you prefer a page a day or a week at a glance. If you plan your working life day-by-day, and need to write in lots of appointments and small tasks, then a page a day, with hours down the side, will be the most useful. If, however, you think in terms of planning a week rather than a day, or you have large blocks of time taken out daily, for example for teaching or clinics, or much of your work is routine, then a week at a glance is probably best.

We'll discuss how to use your diary in the next section.

Information

This section includes everything from the basic – telephone numbers, addresses, conversion charts, maps – to the exotic – where to eat, Christmas present lists . . . You can have a section for finance, for expenses forms, a pocket to collect receipts, bills and so on (and so avoid problems claiming expenses or filling in your taxes), forms to enter credit card purchases and pockets to hold cheque and credit cards. These can also carry business cards and any identification cards you need in your working life.

Your needs will determine the development of this section. None of the commercially available systems have a section printed 'shopping', yet this is invaluable for a shopping list as well as a note of specialist shops or new places to try. If there are people who you are involved with on projects, but don't see on a frequent basis, then pages headed with their name are useful: meetings or phone calls become more efficient as everything you needed to ask or tell them is in front of you.

System Extras

The two things that are the most useful physical additions to your system are a bring-forward file and a wall chart.

- Use a concertina file as a bring-forward file. In it, keep papers and notes for the weeks or months ahead that are too big for your organizer or you don't need to carry around, reminder slips to check other files and details of one-off events you have to attend. A concertina file at home serves the same purpose and reminders are less likely to get overlooked than curled and yellowing notes pinned to a cork board in the kitchen. Check your file in the last week of every month for the month ahead. Things that are important and require action in the first few days of a month you may prefer to file in the previous month.

- Although I think you're asking for trouble if you try and keep more than one diary (one or other is never up to date), the only exception to this is the family wall chart. This year-planner should be prominently displayed, usually in the kitchen or by the main telephone, and records individual and family activities.

The more sophisticated versions use a different colour for each family member and one colour for the family as a whole. If a car(s) is shared a symbol for who has/wants/expects/needs the car can save a lot of aggravation. As space is limited, the best way of using this is to record absences from home, social events, things that impinge on other family members and the dog's birthday.

An about-to-run-out-of shopping list pinned next to the wall chart, to be filled in by everyone and anyone as they use the near-to-last of something (don't wait until it is the last, by then it's often too late) saves a lot of bother. Put a list low enough down so that even young children can fill it in. Not only does this encourage them to learn good organizational habits from an early age but it gives them practice in writing and spelling.

Children pick up your habits very quickly. One woman reported that at a parent's evening at her son's (age 7) school the teacher commented on how much his writing had improved in recent months. She was too embarrassed to say that he had learnt the best way of ensuring she didn't forget what he thought was important was for him to write Post-it notes which he then stuck on the front of her Filofax. And a father reported his children nagged him until they saw him write their requests/dates/ideas in his organizer where they knew it wouldn't get forgotten or overlooked.

Electronic Systems

The theory is that a pocket-sized computer with all the functions of a personal organizer, plus more, is the answer to time management prayers. In practice, the move to electronic, computerized systems is fairly slow. People either love them or hate them. Even those who love them admit it takes time to enter all your relevant data and to get used to using them.

The number on the market and their add-on extras is ever increasing. Their advantages over a conventional organizer and calculator depends on what machine you buy and what you want to use it for. If nothing else, it means you can write legibly on the move. Whether you want an electronic organizer is as much a matter of personality as organization. If you like gadgets and games it will probably appeal. Also, people who spend a lot of time away from the office will make most use of other features that generally come with these machines when they work on trains, planes or in hotel rooms. Those that plug into a personal computer are the most versatile.

If you are thinking of getting an electronic system you will obviously check your needs against its functions – these include anything from spelling and grammar checks to world clocks and translators. Also think about:

- Size and weight
- 'QWERTY' keyboards versus alphabetical keyboards; if you regularly use a keyboard stay with 'QWERTY' to avoid confusion
- Size of keys – small keys that are close together mean it's difficult to type fast and mistakes are common
- Size of screen – the text rolling across it is fine for notes or a directory, but inconvenient if you are writing a report on a train or plane
- Whether you want a password system
- Checking its backup system

If you use an electronic system:

- Store its contents regularly
- Use it regularly; warnings that batteries are low won't be seen if you ignore it for weeks at a time; always have a spare set of batteries if it uses replaceable ones, or regularly charge rechargeable ones

Controlling Your Day

'Let's fight till six and then have dinner,' said Tweedledum.

LEWIS CARROLL

Getting control of your time in the short-term, whether you plan by the day or the week, means becoming proactive rather than reactive — doing what is important to achieve your goals rather than simply reacting to other people's demands. These are terms which have been around in management circles for some time now, and you may have got fed up hearing them. But have you acted on them? This includes looking at attitudes and beliefs that make you respond in particular ways and will be examined later. For now we will look at the organizational aspects of being able to control your time.

Your time can be divided up into three broad categories: committed time, uncontrolled time and controllable time.

Committed Time

This is time over which you have no control; time which you, or others, have committed to certain activities. Some of these are regular and fixed, others may be one-off and random (but once made cannot/should not be changed). Activities in this category include: meetings, formal appointments with other people such as clients and customers, clinics and surgeries, teaching and lectures, church services, conferences . . .

The rest of your time is uncommitted, and falls into the two remaining parts.

Uncontrolled Time

For some people this makes up a substantial proportion of their working day, the time over which you lose control and can't reasonably expect to get control. It is time when we are engaged in trivial or routine tasks, informal appointments or meetings, chats, sudden requests for information, tasks with short deadlines, emergencies . . . Not all the tasks are trivial, this time can include major activities, but they are characterized by their unexpectedness or lack of real predictability. For example, you have a fairly good idea when a cow will calve, and some idea of whether or not you expect her to have difficulties, but you can't fit it neatly into a convenient time slot. It also includes the kinds of things you know you will have to do sometime (e.g. budgets and reports) but you can't make a start because you don't know the exact form it will take.

Controllable Time

This is the time you carve out of uncontrolled time (or the time which is left over, if you are lucky) during which you work on your major tasks and goals. Included in this time could be: planning, thinking, reflecting, small steps to big goals (those slices of salami) and personal-work goals. This is the time you must protect from daily pressures if you are to move forward. Protecting this time relies to a large extent on two things – your ability to say 'no' and thus preventing other things intruding (see Chapters 7 and 8), and the way you use your diary.

Using Your Diary

What does your diary currently tell you? Usually it records committed time, where you have to be to fulfil certain job, personal or social requirements. It is also a record of what other people want you to do. This is a necessary part of a diary's function, but you must aim to use it as a planning tool, a record of what you want to do (and have to do).

Are you one of those people who see a crowded diary as a sign of 'success'? Do you think 'All those people want to see me – I must be important', 'I'm in on all those meetings – I'll know everything that's going on/I must be important/my opinion is valued' or 'I don't have a minute to myself, so I must be achieving something'.

You may have a 'to do' list tucked into your diary and virtuously believe this is 'planning'. Your diary is the link, the bridge, between the goals and aspirations in your overview section and the achievement of those goals. Bridges can be as elaborate and exotic as London's Tower Bridge or as simple and functional as a plank of wood. Only for Indiana Jones (in *The Last Crusade*) is it an act of faith. The type of job you do plus personal preference will dictate whether you need a plank or a multi-span edifice.

For most people planning and gaining control of a week is easier than planning a day. Although there is more time for things to happen and be added there is also more room to be flexible, to build in slippage (without simply adding extra hours at the weekend). Also, your mood and energy will fluctuate during a week and some days it's just easier to get things done than others.

With experience this sort of planning will become second nature and will require very little time. At first you have to think about it and go through the stages step by step:

1. Decide how many hours you will work (i.e. are contracted to work or are prepared to do, including 'extra' or overtime, e.g. forty hours, forty-five hours a week)
2. Mark in all your committed time – meetings, appointments and so forth; add up the overall time
3. Make a list of all the things that have to be done this week – check your priorities and goals as well as deadlines
4. Estimate (and be ruthlessly realistic) how long each task will take; consult your time log for guidance
5. Add up numbers 2 and 4 above: if this comes in at under whatever you decided in 1, then you stand a chance of winning the battle; if it is well over your hours (and you've been honest and realistic), one of two things is happening. Either (i) you're being asked to do too much or (ii) you're not doing things fast enough – because of incompetency, lack of training and skills, chronic tiredness, perfectionism or similar problems. Don't

immediately assume that it is your fault. Unrealistic expectations from your company about what you can do are common. In this situation no amount of time management skills will solve the problem, which needs to be tackled at source. For now, we will assume you're 'under hours'.

6. Estimate, based on past experience and your time log, how much time is likely to be taken up by 'the unexpected' — emergencies, interruptions, delays, trouble-shooting/fire-fighting, acts of God and mistakes of Man.

7. Add this to the total above: take this total (2+4+6=?) from the total hours you intend to work. Again we'll stay optimistic and assume there is a plus number of hours left. This is the maximum (at the moment) over which you can hope to get control.

   This is the time you're going to block off in your diary to use to advance your long-term goals, to work on your priorities (*note*: some goal advancement will automatically take place under 'has-to-be-done').

8. Look at your week and decide (i) when you are least likely to be hassled/interrupted and (ii) when you are most able to work well and then mark off a block of time. You can label this as you like — different people like to call it 'red time', 'available time', '*A* time'. I like to think of it as 'prime time', as in prime time television when the 'best' (or at least, the most popular) shows are on the air and advertisers pay the most because they are reaching the biggest audience. Depending on the amount of time you're trying to block, the task you want to achieve in it and the type of job you do (in relation to interruptions and so on), you may want to break this prime time into two or more blocks or take it as one.

   Where people most often go wrong is in trying to gain control of *too much time too quickly*. They're greedy and block amounts of time they can't hope to gain control over. Then when they're interrupted, or other things take priority, they say, 'See, I told you it wouldn't work. It's not worth bothering.' If you start realistically small you're much more likely to succeed, and can build up from there. If you've been feeling totally overloaded and out-of-control for months, then getting control — real control that you use — of an hour, or even half an hour, is a major achievement.

9. Write in your blocked time this week what you're going to work on.

10. Now, while you're feeling a glow of satisfaction/virtue/ courage go through the next few weeks and mark off some prime time. At the moment you don't need to know exactly what you'll be doing then — but you do know you'll need the time for something. You can refine the system by having two types of blocked time: one in which you work on personal-work goals and another in which you make sure you have time for urgent/important work-work goals, regardless of whether you see them as important to you or not.

11. You may want to start filling in days/times when the various tasks you have to do in the week will be accomplished. The more detailed you are — '11.10 am: *phone Jane*' — the more chance that your plan will go astray. The main thing, or at least the first thing, is getting a match between hours to be worked and length of time tasks take. Next, make the best use of space in your diary. Like packing anything, a cupboard, suitcase or car, put in the large items first. These are the things to plan and write in if at all possible. The smaller items fill in the gaps, the odd moments, and, as long as they are on your 'to do this week/today' list (3 and 4 combined), they won't get forgotten.

12. The final refinement is a 'bring forward' list, with deadlines and the estimated time the task will take. Should everything go so well you have time 'left over', or something gets cancelled or delayed, your priorities and tasks are ready and waiting for you. There is no more dithering over what needs doing next.

13. Take a few minutes at either the end or the beginning of the day to check through your plan and make sure that you're on course to complete your tasks by the end of the week. Doing it at the end of the day means you can start the next day knowing exactly what it is you're going to do. Sorting it out first thing in the morning means you can take account of anything that has happened overnight — the main computer going down/all the

children developing chicken pox/your boss going into premature labour/the first sunny day of spring . . . Don't do it morning and evening unless you get some special benefit — you only end up duplicating the work. And if you spend any longer than ten minutes you're indulging yourself rather than planning. At the end of the week take a little longer, maybe up to thirty minutes, to plan the next week. It is useful to do this then, even if some things are modified on a Monday morning. Although you may not be working on anything over the weekend, you can mull things over, and you may even come to different conclusions about priorities. Good planning isn't accomplished in a mad rush.

Protecting Prime Time

You must learn to protect prime time. Writing something down makes it much easier to say (as well as realize) you're not free when someone wants to see you or have a meeting. If it was committed time you'd say so ('Sorry, I'm in a meeting' or 'I'm taking my daughter to the dentist'). Prime time is just as important. You may not want to say what you're doing and usually there isn't any need to, but you can say to yourself 'I'm writing a report' or 'I'm working on the outline of my new novel'. These are perfectly valid things to be doing; just because you're doing them alone doesn't mean that they don't count, you have to move them to suit someone else or that you can cram them in at any old time.

Of course, there will be times when you have to let go of prime time: when someone sufficiently senior to you wants to see you or when there's a genuine emergency or when Clint Eastwood calls. At other times it's a matter of choice, as when a high-priority opportunity presents itself. Sometimes you may choose to give up your prime time 'for the greater good', usually to fit in with other people's schedules. Only do this if it's really important, and don't do it often unless you can move the same amount of time somewhere else in the week and not go over your allotted working time.

Don't let trivial interruptions disturb you either. If a colleague sticks his or her head round the door and says 'Are you busy?' don't even say 'yes'! (More on this in Chapter 10.) As time management principles become better known, more and more organizations are recognizing the need for employees at all levels to protect some prime time. If your company or department can organize a visual system which tells others to stay away, this is one of the easiest ways to protect prime time. But if you're going to ask other people to respect your prime time you need to respect theirs.

Protecting your prime time from others can be made easier by setting aside time when you are always available to them. This is especially important if you have had an open door policy in the past and now want to close it on occasions. If you make appointments to see people, particularly if you put them off when you are busy and ask them to come back, make sure you see them. Cancelling leads to people not trusting you and becoming more determined to catch you when they can.

Lastly, you have to protect your blocked time from yourself. You've worked too hard to find this time not to use it for the task you've allocated to it. It doesn't matter whether it's spending an hour working on a new procedure for dealing with nuclear waste or an hour beginning to clear the clutter from the top of your desk. This was your choice, your priority. Don't mess about with something else. This is a time for dealing with things that are important – and there comes a time in many people's lives when the top of their desk is a priority!

Reviewing Plans and Goals

Periodically take time to review your goals and plans, update and modify them as necessary and recommit yourself to them. This overhaul of your 'planner' or decision-making base allows you to check whether you are on course or if you've drifted, and then make adjustments accordingly. You shouldn't need to do this more than once or twice a year. January seems psychologically right and sometime in the summer, possibly at holiday time, fits in with most people's schedules. If you are seriously adrift, develop a corrective strategy, if necessary re-keeping a time log for a short period, or reassess your goals. Maybe you want something different from what you thought.

5

ORGANIZING YOUR ENVIRONMENT

Take from our souls the strain and stress,
And let our ordered lives confess
The beauty of thy peace.
JOHN GREENLEAF WHITTIER

The majority of plans for organizing living or working space are variations of 'a place for everything and everything in its place'. This is a good enough rule, certainly, but it overlooks one vital, individual factor. Some people have more 'everything' than others. It doesn't need a quiz to sort people into 'hoarders' or 'chuckers-out', almost everybody can immediately align themselves with one or other side. I am not about to settle any long-standing marital arguments by saying which is better — the answer depends, as always, on a number of things, including personal preference. At the extremes both cause problems. The real issue depends on (i) whether you know what you've got and (ii) whether you can find it when you need it.

Hoarders and Chuckers-Out

Discussing hoarders and chuckers-out anticipates some issues we'll be covering in the next section — the more psychological reasons why your time management and organization is poor, and what you can do about such problems — but it is necessary to make sense of your attitudes to your environment.

Why do you keep things? To most hoarders this is an almost incomprehensible question, the answer is so obvious. You keep things because you might want them in the future — they will 'come in useful'. Once this decision is made it is applied, indiscriminately, to everything.

Do you have a kitchen drawer full of more plastic and paper bags, short pieces of string, bent and rusted 'ties' for freezer bags than you could use in a lifetime? 'Doesn't everyone?' the inveterate hoarder will reply. Well, actually, no. What about: tins of paint with half-an-inch in the bottom and a thick skin on top; every gas, electricity and telephone bill you've ever received; memos from bosses long gone; empty perfume bottles; a desk drawer full of bent paper clips, tangled elastic bands, unnamed telephone numbers on scraps of paper, dried-up bottles of correcting fluid, a key that doesn't fit any known lock; every painting ever done by your children; out-of-date insurance policies, vaccination papers, guarantees for gadgets you no longer own; minutes for committees you're no longer on; furniture you'll get round to stripping or repairing one day; out-of-date medicine; odd socks or lone earrings; souvenirs from places you hated; gadgets that don't work . . .? You get the general idea.

The first piece of reassurance I'll offer the hoarder is that I'm not suggesting you throw everything out. But you do have to look at why you hoard things before you'll be able to make sensible decisions about what to keep and what has to go. Most reasons fall into one of the following broad categories:

Useful

- 'I'll need it in the future': it might be genuinely useful in the not-too-distant future, but people tend to anticipate their future needs very generously
- 'It'll do if the main one breaks down': keeping something for second best can sometimes be justified, but if you're replacing it, why? If it's faulty/dangerous/worn out what good will it be when it's needed? If there is nothing wrong with it you're probably hanging on it to assuage the guilt of buying an unnecessary new one. And how likely is breakdown?
- 'I'm keeping it for spare parts': this might be justified, but be ruthlessly realistic
- 'It might be worth something': find out what it's worth now and estimate what it might be worth in the future (in five years? Ten?

Fifty?) Is it worth the effort of keeping until then?

Reassurance

- 'I might need it': it makes you feel safe to have things to hand, but how many empty yoghurt pots do you really need?
- Keeping up with the Jones's: covetousness, acquiring new and unnecessary things, having to have the most up-to-date/expensive model can be used to bolster poor self-esteem
- 'Proof that I did something': sensible if it's your current inoculation status or examination certificates, otherwise it bolsters a flagging ego or is sentimental (see below)
- It conveys an image: a wall full of books makes you feel intellectual even if you never open any of them, and a shelf of cookery books makes you feel domestic even if everything you eat comes out of cans
- Old love letters reassure you you were loved, or letters from friends say nice things about you . . .
- Throwing something out sometimes means admitting we made a mistake in what we bought/made/collected/obtained and this can be difficult. The longer you've had something the easier it should be to acknowledge that your taste/value system/judgement/needs have changed.

Sentimentality

- 'It was a present': it was given with love and that compels you to keep it. Why? Remember the giver, and the thought, and accept that you don't have to keep everything they give you. If you think you clutter other people up, resolve to give usable presents.
- It's a way of remembering a person, place or event: if you like it, use it or enjoy it, fine. Otherwise, why are you keeping it? Could you remember without it?
- 'Proof I did something': coming second in the wheelbarrow race is the highlight of your sporting career . . .?

- 'It's a family heirloom': does it have other worth such as cash value, aesthetic value or important family history associations, or is it simply 'old junk'?

Aesthetics

- 'I like clutter': this is not to do with fashionableness but a matter of personal style – baroque versus classical or Russian Orthodox versus Shaker

Aspirational

- 'I'll need it when we move to the country/retire/get a second home/decorate the bedroom/take up patchwork': how realistic is this?
- 'I'm creative – I need clutter': do you, or is it about creating an image?

Greed and Possessiveness

- 'It's mine and I won't give it up': even to the dustbin?
- 'Everyone else has one, so I must have one': see also reassurance
- 'If I keep it no one else can have it': someone else having it somehow diminishes you
- 'It's too nice to use': surely one of the silliest reasons for keeping something

Habit

- 'My mother kept it, so I keep it': enough said!

Some of these reasons are perfectly valid, and others are at least acceptably human. What is wrong with being sentimental? Greed is more questionable. Recognizing why you keep so much 'junk' is a preliminary to sorting it out, but beware of rationalizations masquerading as legitimate reasons. As we all become more environmentally aware it makes sense to recycle whenever possible, but be realistic both in recognizing the potential of what you are keeping and your potential to use it. Keeping a few foil containers from Indian take-aways, glass jars or whatever for your next DIY project is fine; you don't need a cupboard full. Isn't it more 'green' to use something until it wears out than to keep it as 'second best' while you find another excuse to buy the latest model? If you can't bring yourself to throw disposables away don't use them. How good a use of the earth's resources is it to live in a large house (which has to be heated, cleaned and otherwise maintained) just to hold your collection of potentially recyclable junk? One of the worst cases of hoarding I've come across is a woman who saves old batteries because 'they look all right'!

Some people will always feel uncomfortable without masses of 'things' around them. Other people prefer monastic aestheticism. If you use it or enjoy it then keep it. What you should get rid of are things which don't fall into either category, but must be stored, looked after, cleaned, moved around, possibly insured and protected and get in the way of things you use and love. Remember Pareto's principle: you almost certainly get 80 per cent of your fun/use/information/value from 20 per cent of your possessions. If your sense of self-worth *only* comes from what you own this is a matter for a therapist, not time management.

There are only two real problems that 'chuckers-out' are likely to experience (apart from living with someone they consider a hoarder). One is 'the baby going out with the bath water' so to speak. Most are philosophically resigned to this happening some time and see it as the lesser of two evils. A modicum of forward thinking is, however, essential to prevent this. The other problem is a refusal to keep anything because you won't re-use it, even when appropriate. 'New' comes to mean 'best' and this is likely to have a lot to do with seeking reassurance and bolstering a sagging ego. When an antique dining table gets labelled 'old', 'new' has probably come to mean 'clean' and you might be showing signs of obsessional behaviour to do with cleanliness.

Clearing Out

> *What, after all,*
> *Is a halo? It's only one more thing to keep clean.*
> CHRISTOPHER FRY

Every year we are reminded 'a dog is for life, not just for Christmas', but there is no need to apply this worthy precept to everything we acquire. Not everything is for life. Whether you need a clear-out of junk at home or at work (although for hoarders it is likely to be both) the same basic guidelines apply:

- Set time aside: Although routine filing can be slotted into odd moments, major sorting and clearing takes time. Some people like the 'blitz' idea – taking a day and thoroughly 'doing' the place – and are rewarded by that immensely satisfying emotion of smug virtue. This is a good idea if you (i) can really get it all done and (ii) don't run out of energy, enthusiasm and courage. Major clearing-out can be physically, psychologically and emotionally tiring, as one decision after another is made and then requires large items being moved around. If you have a lifetime's worth of junk to sort, a jungle to tame rather than a gentle weeding of the herbaceous border, then you're better to set aside one or two hours at a time and do as much as you can in that time. If you have open-ended clearing time you're likely to get fed-up before you finish.

  If necessary, and it's possible, go into work for a half day on a Saturday or Sunday for a good sort out. You'll feel less guilty about 'wasting time' when you should be working and you won't have to put up with the 'advice', comments or jokes of colleagues. Nor will you have to feel furtive or embarrassed about just how much you're getting rid of.

- Break the task up: If you can't get everything done in one go and you feel a couple of hours won't make any difference to the general mess, break the task up – your desk top/the drawers in the sideboard/the kitchen cupboards/A to L in the filing cabinet/the garden shed . . . In the midst of total chaos a clean, neat, tidy cupboard, 'de-junked', stands like a beacon of hope and inspiration. It also proves you can do it, when you put your mind, and the time, to it.

- Frame of mind: Try not to have a clear-out if you're unhappy, fed-up or depressed unless past experience has taught you that it cheers you up (it can, demonstrating you have some control over your life/you've accomplished something useful/you feel virtuous and so on). Otherwise it's more likely to leave you feeling even worse. You'll probably make unwise decisions and either end up keeping everything or throwing everything out, even that which you could have kept. Background music which maintains your spirits and wards off boredom is a big help, no matter whether it's the Beach Boys or Beethoven, Madonna or Mozart.
- Wear old clothes: So getting dirty and dusty doesn't matter. Even in your office clearing out years of accumulated papers is surprisingly dirty work. Don't wear anything with big pockets that you can put things in 'just in case'.
- Have a sufficient supply of rubbish bags: It's extremely frustrating to be in the full swing of throwing out and to run out.
- Have a good plan of how you're going to store things and where everything is to go (which we'll discuss in the next section).
- Make sensible decisions: Be realistic about why you're keeping things. Does everybody in the office need to have complete sets of minutes or can one central set be used? Are you keeping out-dated information? Are you keeping things you could easily get elsewhere? If necessary refer back to the earlier section on why you keep things. Just how many security blankets do you need?
- Get help: Sometimes help is needed both to make decisions and physically move things, but there are many decisions only you can make. Don't ask someone to help make the decisions if you're going to end up blaming them for making the wrong one.
- Maintain courage: It's hard at first to let things go, to give up things you've been hanging on to for years. Sometimes you even find a use for something you threw out the week before. But

before berating yourself, ask: (i) did you know you had it before you found it to throw out?; (ii) did you think of a use for it simply because you'd seen it?; and (iii) how hard have you been trying to convince yourself it was all a mistake so you don't have to do any more clearing out?

• The minute you find yourself retrieving something you've just made a decision to throw away, stop. You've lost your critical edge.

To Keep or Not To Keep

. . . is a much more pertinent question to the inveterate hoarder, let the philosophers worry about being. When cleaning out bear in mind the three *R*s — retain, reject or repair. These are the only decisions you can make, and they need to be made with the fourth *R* — ruthlessly. Ruth is the quality of compassion, of pity and need not be applied to yellowing memos/rusted and bent nails/threadbare pullovers/photographs of headless people/perfectly good but crippling shoes/unattractive postcards from people you've forgotten/a 1985 restaurant guide/aftershave you hate/books you should read, but won't . . .

Accept that things age and die (and deserve burial or cremation). Not everything can be repaired. If it's old and worn out let it go. If it's new and broken get it repaired. Don't hang on to it in the hope that it might be repairable. That's akin to having your body frozen in the hope that in the future they'll be able to cure you. By the time they can you'll be an anachronism in an alien world.

Most of us have a tendency to allow a fourth pile to accumulate — a 'maybe' pile: maybe it'll be useful, maybe I'll want it, maybe it's repairable, maybe it'll come back into fashion (bellbottoms and kipper ties don't even deserve an honourable burial), maybe I'll lose weight, maybe I'll find someone who will want it . . .

The problem is often one of feeling guilty about throwing things away, but the choice is straightforward — dump it, or find it a good home. If it's broken (beyond repair), worn out or generally useless, accept the fact. Don't send clothes that won't even make good dusters to a jumble sale. If it's usable, in reasonable condition, worth something and you no longer have a use for it or no longer like it then find it a home. You have two options. You could sell it or give it away. Sell it (through classified ads, auction houses, postcards in shop windows, second-hand shops or car-boot sales) if it is worth something and you need/want the money. Often the money you get hardly seems worth the effort, so you hang on to it and do nothing. Or, be generous, give it to a worthy cause. There can hardly be a community which doesn't have a charity shop. Take good quality things to them and help others while you help yourself towards a tidier home. Some groups, such as hostels for the homeless or battered women, will take adult's and children's clothes, toys and sometimes furniture for immediate redistribution. Check these out locally. Jumble sales will take virtually anything, but don't send them what really belongs in the bin. Dump it yourself. You can check with friends and family whether they want something before you get rid of it, but don't use emotional blackmail ('it was your grandmother's') to foist things you don't want onto others.

If your reject pile remains at little more than a battered pair of slippers or a set of minutes from a now defunct committee which only met twice, apply less ruth. If being morbid helps, imagine how you would feel if you were to drop dead and your colleagues or family had to come in and clear out after you – now. Do you want an obituary which records you as being survived by twenty-four empty margarine containers/a tattered collection of Elvis posters/sixteen assorted lipsticks/every birthday card you ever received/minutes from every meeting you ever attended/four unfinished kit models/tins of rusty nails and screws/a rotting pile of elderly T-shirts/a pile of newspapers dating back five years/more shoes than Imelda Marcos ... ?

What you are left with is a pile of useful or beautiful things – the things you know you will take pleasure from, which will ease your life. What are you going to do with them?

Storage

Losing things is not always related to hoarding. True, you can keep so much that you can never find what you want when you want it (which is the same as losing it) but poor storage and neglect of priorities contribute to loss.

It is only now that you have cleared out much of the junk in your life that you need to think about how and where you are going to organize and store it. To have done so before would have meant planning for much more storage space than you actually need. Sometimes, less is less. Your storage system, whether at home or at work, needs to be simple to use, otherwise you'll give up on it. Personal taste and budget play a part, but largely in relation to externals. Job or family requirements have more impact, but now that you've got rid of excess garbage 'a place for everything and everything in its place' makes more sense. You should aim to be able to lay your hands on whatever you want in no more than a couple of minutes, excluding, maybe, getting into the attic/archives.

Before you launch into a frenzy of packing everything away take time to develop your system, step-by-step, otherwise you'll end up with everything out of sight and no idea where it is.

1. List all your storage areas (the more space you have the more you will keep), and designate them active, that is easily accessible, or inactive, the more remote, harder-to-reach places. The shorter you are, unfortunately, the more inaccessible places there are. We're talking about everything from the cupboard under the stairs to the top of the wardrobe, built-in bookshelves to magazine racks, your in-tray to the company's archives.
2. Approach the task with an open, divergent, flexible mind. True, keeping your clothes in the bedroom and the best china in the dining room is appropriate, but who's to know (or care) that you have files stored in the drawer under the bed? In a properly ventilated bathroom you can keep bookshelves full of books. In one very upmarket church-conversion-to-small-flats, the communal laundry room doubles as a library, where people keep

their paperbacks and borrow from one another.

3. Assess how much something is used and plan your space accordingly. Things that are used daily need to be in obvious, easily accessible places. Things used once or twice a year can go in the hard-to-reach places. Bulky things need to find a home first.

4. Take a lesson from the Shakers and hang everything you can on the walls. A clear floor automatically makes a place look tidier. The Shakers even hung their chairs. Hang things as high as reachably possible, or have floor to ceiling shelves and a good pair of steps.

5. Don't overcrowd your storage space. If you can't see what you've got you'll forget it. The more things you have to move in a cupboard to get something out the more likely there are to be breakages, and the less likely you are to put something back. Clothes come out crumpled and require re-ironing, papers get tangled and torn and need resorting.

6. Don't put things away with the idea of going back and re-sorting. Exercise control at the outset – you'll never get back to it.

7. Exercise restraint in gadgets to keep you organized – often they only help you store more junk. Pegboards for frequently used tools or kitchen equipment are excellent, numerous desk tidies are dubious.

8. While it might be useful to label seldom seen boxes in attics with their contents, a system which requires instructions and lists on a daily basis will soon fall by the wayside. Use cardboard boxes sparingly; when you can't see what is in them you're more likely to forget; they need careful labelling if you're not to end up going through them all. One useful box can be labelled 'sentimental rubbish' – it means exactly what it says, things of personal, sentimental value to you and no one else. A box keeps it all together, means you can enjoy an occasional orgy of nostalgia and it is easily stored out of the way the rest of the time.

9. Storage space needs good lighting – garages, sheds and cupboards that are too dim make for inefficient use and cause accidents.

10. Make storage space as easy to keep clean as possible by using appropriate materials.
11. Make your storage areas clear to everyone and do not use inappropriate places for storage. This story of a postgraduate student should be enough to deter you. Not being well organized, and having lots of papers relating to a research project scattered across his desk and the surrounding floor, he needed somewhere to balance several files of original data. The nearest available space was the top of the wastepaper basket. In the middle of the night he remembered he had left them there . . . but it was too late and six months of data collection was nothing more than a charred memory in the hospital incinerator.

If your storage system fails you and you still can't find things you have two options. The first, a folk remedy, is to tie a red ribbon to the leg of a chair which is supposed to bring a lost object back, or offer up a prayer to St Anthony, patron saint of the lost.

Working Space

In the best designed kitchens it is easy to move from sink to food preparation area to stove to serving area in a neat progression with everything within arm's reach. There should be no need for excess walking and movement – no crossing the room with pans of boiling water. Any good working space should be designed for efficiency and economy of movement, but don't get obsessive about it. You can't work in the same position all the time without getting cramp, or stiff, or tense. Getting up and moving around the office occasionally to collect paper or get a file may be a useful change of posture rather than a wasted minute. Having to get up to answer your telephone every five minutes *is* a waste of time.

The organization of your working space depends very much on your job and your company and whether you have your own office or are in open plan space. Since you may have very little control over many things you need to exercise control where you can.

Your Desk

Research claims that the average executive or office worker wastes approximately thirty minutes a day with the jumble of papers on their desk, trying to find things, being distracted or moving it about when it collapses or to find more space. That adds up to a least fourteen working days a year. Imagine that time spent on your pet project, or on holiday.

Almost every time management book or course reiterates the idea that 'a cluttered desk is the sign of a cluttered mind'. I am tempted to ask what an empty desk is the sign of? Jumping to these easy, clichéd conclusions based on making links between externals can be detrimental to change (see Chapter 8). You may strenuously deny the cluttered desk-cluttered mind link, feeling comfortable with your clutter. Other people may call you disorganized, you may prefer to describe yourself as non-organizationally oriented. It is only a problem if you can't find things when you need them, you get distracted from the task in hand and you have no room left in which to work. These all waste time. If, however, your desk is cluttered in the eyes of others (even your own) but you can find everything you want quickly, you still have space to work and you genuinely don't get distracted by the mounds of paper, then the only problem is that other people will still probably perceive you as messy, inefficient, even poor at making decisions. If this is going to damage your credibility a modicum of order is called for.

What reasons do people give for a cluttered desk?

- 'Out of sight, out of mind': Keeping a pile of papers on your desk is no guarantee that you'll remember what or why something is there, or when it has to be done. Keep papers filed away and use your organizer as your memory. Despite popular belief, important papers do not work themselves to the top of the pile (nor do they spontaneously compost).
- 'I'm creative, clutter is important': Some creative people do use clutter to stimulate themselves. New combinations appear,

colours, shapes, ideas, objects. It only becomes a problem if it also prevents you working because you can't find anything, including space. It is, however, more frequently a rationalization than a truth.

- 'I like clutter' — as a matter of aesthetics: A Spartan desk makes you feel anxious, intimidated.
- 'I'm a busy person, clutter is inevitable': Just as some people equate a full diary with being important, so some (probably the same) people believe a cluttered desk shows how productive they are. It is more likely to convey the opposite impression.
- 'I don't have time to clear up': Faced with the figures in the first paragraph, how do you not have time?
- 'It's not my job': You've always had a mother, wife or servant picking up after you and you see lifting a finger to look after yourself as beneath you. Clearing your desk isn't macho.

The top of your desk is for working on, not a storage space. The best way of gaining control of your desk is a good filing system, which is properly used and gets as much out of sight as possible. Look at what you keep on your desk: telephone/Dictaphone/desk tidy (complete with four ballpoint pens in different colours, three unsharpened pencils, a dried-up highlighter pen, ruler, scissors, paper clips, elastic bands, pins . . .)/in-tray/out-tray/stationery tidy (with forms, compliment slips, envelopes . . .)/blotter/word processor, typewriter or computer/piles of correspondence/three half-full cups of cold coffee/journals and magazines/the sign with your name on it/address file/catalogue system/dead plant/remains of an apple/customer or client files/note pads/reps' give-away gimmicks and freebies/hole punch/stapler/Sellotape dispenser/ paperweight/receipts for expenses/framed photograph of your family/multiple piles of random papers/manufacturers' samples/ half-eaten sandwich/indigestion tablets/note reminding you to buy bread, wine, toilet rolls . . .

What isn't on top of your desk out of this lot is in a jumble in the drawers. What is essential on your desk? Cut the equipment down to a minimum. If it's not a main tool of your job can your word processor or computer have its own desk or trolley? If you get a lot of back, neck or wrist ache when you use it you're probably in the wrong position anyway (see Chapter 13). Have your telephone on your non-dominant side (for most, the left) so that you can hold it in this hand and write with the other, if necessary. Since we read from left to write you will be most comfortable working in that direction (although a few left-handers may want to reverse this). Organize your equipment/resources in the order you need them, from left to right and with the most used nearest to hand. If you have your in-tray on the left of your desk and your out-tray on the right you can imagine a line down the centre of the desk and aim to keep everything moving left to right and not backwards.

Try to get everyone to put everything in your in-tray rather than leaving notes on your desk, chair or places where they can be overlooked or lost. Centrally gathered in-trays or pigeon holes are useful, especially if everyone is in the habit of emptying them frequently. Your in-tray should never be full but should be frequently emptied and decisions made as a result.

Having cleared your desk of clutter you then have space for what you actually need to work with. Don't keep piles of paper 'in case' or 'to remind me'. If this sounds impossibly sterile gather your papers together in labelled files. Transparent plastic files are very convenient as you can see at a glance what is in them. A neat, small pile of files is less offensive to other people's sense of clutter than a haphazard, toppling pile of loose paper. Anything which enables you to like and use a system rather than discard it as boring is to be encouraged — colour coding, using files, paper, tags, paper clips or whatever; use one of your interesting pots for pencils and a decorative box for your elastic bands and paper clips; pin interesting things on your memo board to provide an ever-changing visual display (and it gets it off your desk). Do whatever makes you feel more comfortable but doesn't detract from use.

For an ongoing project that requires lots of paper, charts, computer printouts or articles to be gathered around you while you work, have another desk set for this if at all possible. If you don't have a second desk, can you extend your desk with a small table or otherwise create additional space? It can save so much time not having to keep getting things out and putting them away. It also means you can make use of short amounts of time to work on the project. One woman who makes hand-sewn patchwork quilts (each taking hundreds of hours) says a lot of the work is done in 'odd ten or twenty minutes'. This is because the work is never 'tidied away' but left by her chair so that it can be picked up and worked on at any time.

To do this requires (i) a tolerance of some clutter, (ii) the knowledge that it isn't going to sit untouched for five weeks, (iii) adequate space and (iv) only one project like this at a time. More than one means your desk will be back to tottering piles within a few days.

Paperwork

Sometime in the 1970s we were promised the paperless office. Technology would make the written word obsolete. Only in science fiction has this come true. (How often do you see a piece of paper in *Star Trek*?) In fact, technology has generated more paper – faxes, computer printouts, spread sheets, photocopies. And in a world of information overload, articles, memos, journals, magazines, reports and reviews multiply. I often feel the person who invented the photocopier should be hanged, drawn and quartered – nearly as often as I think he should be canonized.

Most of us acquire more paper than we need or know what to do with. Much of it is generated by others, but a lot comes from our need to acquire information. Things may be clutter, but we rarely consider information clutter. How can information, knowledge, facts or opinions be junk? Ask yourself why you need it and assess your answers using the same categories as before (see also Chapter 11). Some is useful, a lot is reassurance, or even greed. Waiting for more information is a good excuse to delay action. When possible, manage paper by not collecting it in the first place.

Most of us open our mail, glance at the contents, put it down, glance at the next one, and so on. This, we believe, gives us an 'overview' from which we make decisions about priorities. True, but it also means we handle each piece of paper more often than we need.

For a truly frightening exercise in self-knowledge the only equipment you need is a red felt tip pen (or something similar which leaves a clear, easily seen, unambiguous mark). Every time you pick up a piece of paper put a dot in the top corner. If, after half an hour your desk looks as though bubonic plague has broken out you know where your time is going. Make decisions about paper. There are five basic choices, which I've summarized as:

DRAFT

D: Do it
R: Refer it
A: Put it in Abeyance
F: File it
T: Throw it away

Do It

A matter can be urgent and important, urgent and trivial, important and non-urgent, necessary (but not important) and non-urgent. Assess categories by your priorities and space available in your daily or weekly plan. To aid the 'doing', and so you don't keep picking up the same pieces of paper, use a desk file system. Use transparent plastic files and/or clear labelling. Basic files are: do now/urgent, do soon and working files for current projects. Files in this last group are not the same as storage files. They contain papers needed immediately, not the last five years correspondence. The really active 'do now' files will always be in use, the others can be kept in your desk drawer if it takes hanging files or if there are few enough to stack. If your desk doesn't have drawers deep enough try adding a two-drawer filing cabinet at the side.

You can use the same system at home with an active file holding unpaid bills, bank and credit card statements for checking and so forth.

Refer It

This includes work to be delegated (see Chapter 10), things that are outwith your area of authority or responsibility (you can refer up as well as down).

Abeyance

This is the middle-of-the-road decision and the one which causes most problems. There may be legitimate reasons for delaying something – you genuinely need more information or a decision from elsewhere, it is non-urgent and low priority, or it is trivial and you believe if you ignore it it will be forgotten about with no negative consequences.

All this can go into the desk filing system or your bring-forward concertina file. Either put reading with the appropriate project or create a 'to read' file. If you intend to work at home have a 'take home' file into which everything goes, so at the end of the day you simply pick it up without having to hunt through a pile of papers trying to remember what there is and making more decisions.

There are, however, inappropriate delaying decisions which we usually call procrastination and which will be discussed in Chapter 7.

File It

As well as your desk file you need a permanent filing system, but remember that just because something is stored alphabetically doesn't guarantee it isn't junk. Decide what you genuinely have to keep, checking company guidelines, rules or legal requirements if necessary. Is there a central storage area where inactive files go? Do both you and your secretary keep copies of the same thing? Why? If you don't have to use a standard company filing system develop the simplest system which works best for you. Take advice from your secretary and if you don't have one try to find one who will give you some advice.

The two main methods are alphabetical, by name, or by subject. Some jobs require a filing system first organized by geography, first by region or country, then sub-regions. An index or list of files is used like a contents table. It can save you creating many similar files (if you use subjects) and means that, should it be necessary, other people can make use of your filing system, either to file for you or find things.

Cross-referencing is a refinement to save creating multiple copies of something which could be filed in several places, or many files which overlap. Whilst cross-referencing can be important and useful it can easily get out of hand and become cumbersome and time-consuming.

Of course, you will file-as-you-go and not let it accumulate, but there are a few other guidelines to easier filing (although it always remains boring):

- Put recent information in the front
- Attach copies of replies to original letters
- Use staples – paper clips fall off, pins stab the unwary
- Don't let the miscellaneous file grow too big; when five or six items have collected start a file for them. If you can't decide where to file something, and it doesn't warrant a new file question whether you really need to keep it.
- If you know when something can be thrown away write the date on the top. Weeding out then becomes automatic, as you see a 'throw-by' date you throw it. No decision.
- Fold paper so the important name/title shows
- Don't overcrowd files or drawers; leave enough space for easy access
- If you, or anyone else, remove something, whether the whole file or a piece of paper, put in a card showing name of the person with the material and date
- When you put something back in a file, put it back in order (where the marker is) rather than just shoving it in the front
- Remember that fax messages deteriorate over time: if the document is important take a photocopy and store that. Also, there is some debate as to whether a fax is a legal document –

the original of a signed contract is legally more sound than a fax of the same contract.
- A good filing system at home is as important as one in the office. A category for each person is useful which includes all their documentation — health, education, employment record, with certificates and so on; also, one for the car, any pets, the house, including insurance, guarantees and receipts, tax documents, and a general money file. Or, have a system which keeps all like things together, such as insurance documents.

Throw it Away

Make friends with your wastepaper basket. Ask yourself why you're keeping something. Is it really necessary? Ask yourself 'what's the worst thing that will happen if I throw it away?' Tear things up, yes it takes seconds longer, but it makes retrieval more difficult and while you're learning to throw things out it gives a wonderful sense of release and a demonstration of your control over the paper and not its control of you.

Layout and Furnishings

In most offices you have little control over this, but where possible consider the basic points:

- Lighting should be adequate, from behind you, not over-harsh and adjustable to your needs
- Arrange your desk so it doesn't encourage interruptions, for example so it doesn't face the door
- Have things that are frequently used in easy reach of your desk
- Get rid of distracting clutter but keep that which makes you feel good/inspires creativity/lightens your soul
- Get a comfortable, adjustable chair at the appropriate height
- Have enough surface space to hold necessary equipment —

computer screen, keyboard and printer, telephone . . .

Working at Home

If you run your business from home you will have adequate space set aside for it and an organized system (I sincerely hope). People who bring work home in the evening and weekends have more of a problem. Always try and keep your work in one place, for your own sanity and your family's. You can't expect to work in peace and quiet in the living room if this is where the family television is. Spreading work about can also cause associations with work all over the house and make you feel guilty when you're not working. One research student reported spending more and more time in the bathroom because he 'felt comfortable there'. What he quickly realized was that in every other room in his small flat there were piles of questionnaires, computer print-outs and other reminders of his research project. Simply catching sight of them was enough to make him feel guilty he wasn't working.

Having one place to work also means you're more likely to become conditioned to working there and it will be easy to start, rather than messing around pretending you're working. The same rules of organized space, avoidance of unnecessary clutter, efficient filing and so forth apply.

Some people choose to work at home to avoid interruptions in the office, but don't create your own interruptions. It can give you a sense of efficient use of time if, when you take a break to make coffee, you load the washing machine while you're waiting for the water to boil. It is a waste of time if you don't get down to work because you've been doing chores/reading the paper before you start/are interrupted by children, partner, neighbours, the dog.

Portable Work Environment

What do you bring home from work? Many people carry huge

amounts of paperwork backwards and forwards on a daily basis in that instrument of torture, the briefcase. Use it sensibly:

- Decide realistically whether you will do any work and how much
- Decide what you want to work on and only carry what is necessary for that. Forget the origins of the word briefcase and concentrate on 'brief' as in 'little'. It's demoralizing to carry things backwards and forwards that don't get touched.
- Don't carry a lot 'in case' – if you haven't decided which of several things you need to work on you have to sort out your priorities, not carry more
- Keep a 'to do' file in your briefcase – short, trivial tasks, reading or correspondence – which is always to hand when you have a spare minute out of your office
- For work which requires a lot of paper, books, print-outs, data or articles, try to keep the work in one place and only work there; the more you carry things about the more opportunities you create to forget/lose/mislay/misfile/get-fed-up-with them.

As well as a bag for carrying things in, a briefcase acts as a status symbol, image-maker or portable office. If you do a lot of work on planes, trains or in waiting areas, then a sturdy, flat-sided case makes the best portable desk, and usually has compartments inside to hold stationery and office equipment. People who want to create an impression of being busy and important will carry bulging briefcases (often more than one) overflowing with papers. They are fooling no one and are more likely to look disorganized, indecisive or inefficient. To carry a small suitcase to and from work on a daily basis creates derision rather than respect. The cautious will want combination locks and the paranoid a briefcase which is bomb-proof and fire resistant. Few of us need a briefcase such as James Bond's in *From Russia With Love* which was weighted down with hidden blades, gold sovereigns and exploding tear gas canisters.

6

SAVE MINUTES ... SAVE HOURS

But meanwhile it is flying, irretrievable time is flying.

VIRGIL

In seeking to manage their time better some people get hung up on doing everything faster, finding the quickest way, taking short cuts, using time-saving gadgets and cutting out anything that is deemed 'a waste of time'. Although many things can be speeded up, often the time saved is seconds or a few minutes. Even if it becomes the odd hour, what is the good of this unless you use the time saved wisely — that is to further your goals (including fun and relaxation)?

Many of us have grown up with the adage 'look after the pennies and the pounds will look after themselves'. Just as this is not the best way to budget and save money, and can make you look penny-pinching in the extreme, so too can seeking to save minutes make you look cold, joyless, uncaring and unconcerned about interacting with the people around you. When saving money, cutting out the little luxuries is often harder, more disheartening and less effective than reassessing your whole budget and making one major cut. Gaining control over your time depends more on understanding your priorities and planning than juggling odd minutes. Having said that, there are habits you can change, new behaviours you can adopt or general guidelines you can follow, which save you small pieces of time, and this can make you feel you are progressing, even while you sort out the bigger issues.

Coupled with this is making good use of odd, fragmented bits of time. This is a particular problem for those at home looking after young children, but encompasses travelling, being kept waiting and no-show appointments. Good use of an unexpected hour is as important as good planning.

There is one caveat I would add: don't make saving time such a priority that you give up doing something you love, or in a way that gives you pleasure, for the gain of a few minutes. Let me give you a personal example.

I make patchwork quilts and have done so seriously (that is, it is extremely important to me) since I was 12. I use the English method which, without getting technical, involves cutting out paper templates as well as material, tacking the material over the papers which then have to be removed when the pieces have been oversewn together. This is much more time-consuming than the American method which dispenses with papers and joins the fabric with a running stitch. I won't even think about machining! What is important is that I enjoy the method I use. I like the quilts I make but the process of making them is as important as the finished object. There seems no point in speeding up the process for the sake of it. If I were making quilts for a living then I might need to think about streamlining the process. It has saddened me at various quilt meetings when women have said that they liked the English method but had given it up on the advice of teachers who had said 'it takes too long', and use a technique with which they are less happy.

Saving time is not always the best thing you can do for yourself. Sometimes allowing yourself the time to enjoy the process is as important as attaining the end result. Efficiency shouldn't turn into overload.

Habits

- Do one thing at a time. Anything that requires thought or concentration or is important should have your whole attention. Talking to someone on the telephone and writing a letter simultaneously does not save time if you make mistakes/mishear and need something repeating/give the other person the impression you're disinterested or going senile. A task carried out with your whole concentration and energy will usually be faster and easier and leave you feeling better about it.

- Double up. Where activities don't require your total concentration you can combine them, so long as safety isn't compromised. Combine them sensibly. Very little television requires total concentration and can easily be combined with other tasks, such as your exercise bike. Doing the ironing can be combined with listening to foreign language tapes whereas negotiating the rush-hour traffic is not the best time to be learning a new skill.
- Do something once. How much time do you waste going back to something because you didn't do it properly/make the decision the first time round.

  Take cutting articles from the newspaper, which many of us do (although after the last chapter I hope you're reassessing how much you keep and why). Do you read the newspaper, decide there is something worth keeping, put it on one side and then go back to it, which usually involves further reading as you glance at articles a second time or read things you didn't bother with the first time round?

  The obvious thing to do is to cut them out as you read. But . . . someone will be saying . . . other people want to read the paper after me. If so, could you possibly read the paper second? (If that idea horrifies you, maybe you need to consider why.) The next best solution is to mark clearly with a coloured pen or highlighter (blue and black ink and pencil gets lost) what you want to save then you can quickly go back and find these without having to re-read even the headlines. You can combine this with watching television/listening to music. Even better, you can persuade (bribe) one of your children to do the cutting for you. Don't ask your secretary to do it unless you are certain she has time, the clippings are entirely work related and the task is defined within her job description. And unless you file them straight away in a readily accessible system why are you bothering?
- File ideas/clippings. There's no point in keeping ideas or clippings if you don't know where they are. They are easy to keep in slip-in folders. Label them to suit your circumstances – for

example DIY/shops/local places of interest (for use in school holidays or for visitors)/health/financial.

- Make the best use of your video if you have one by recording programmes and watching them when you want to. We do this automatically when we go out, but what about when we stay in? If you want to work in the early evening, video programmes and watch them later. If you're feeling alert why sit in front of the television when you could be doing something which requires more of you? It's easy to waste odd half-hours between interesting programmes. Either have a half-hour task/activity planned or video one programme and eliminate the gap.

- Read instructions. People waste time because they assume they know how something works and don't bother to read the instructions. Save time, your temper and possibly broken gadgets by reading, and following, instructions — before you try it your way.

- Get small labels printed with your name, home address and telephone number and use them. This is particularly important if your writing isn't as legible as others would like it to be. Get a stamp or labels printed for work too. Even if you have to pay it is worth it.

- Write important dates (such as birthdays or anniversaries) in your diary in a bright colour that you don't use for anything else. This means they leap out at you and don't get overlooked. It also makes transferring them easier each year.

- Audio tapes can be used practically anywhere, but to successfully learn from them requires some planning. Learning from a tape is not entertainment, the ideas won't just transmit themselves to you during one playing. If you are used to listening to music on tapes, for example in the car, to switch to something to learn, be it a language or management skills, requires a different frame of mind. Read the support material which comes with the tape so you know what's happening. Play the tape through once so you get an overall view, then go back over it as many times as necessary. Then make notes. Tapes which go with books can help you decide whether you want to read the book or reinforce the main points after you have read it.

Skills

Are there skills you could develop to improve your use of time? Depending on your job/present talents consider:

- Memory training
- Speed reading
- Speed writing or shorthand
- Typing
- Report writing
- Learning to use specialist software packages
- Learning to drive
- Public speaking
- Assertiveness
- Communication skills

Technology

- Technology doesn't replace people. Some companies have got so hooked on the idea that computers can do it all that they've tried to get rid of clerical staff and found that managers get bogged down in clerical duties – not just on the computer but filing, photocopying and faxing. If you can't re-hire, check what you're doing and why. What can go? Invest in sensible training so that you (and other relevant staff) know the software and all the short-cuts it can offer.
- Some gadgets certainly save time, there is no denying that, but others are questionable. An automatic washing machine is one of progress's greatest gifts. Although the invention of the washing machine reduced the hours and energy spent manually pummelling washing and hefting it between boiler, sink, mangle and washing line it also changed our attitudes. As washing has

become easier we wash things more often – sometimes to the extent of losing some of the time we should have saved, and perhaps being a little wasteful of our resources. Think of the word processor and how easy it is to make changes. How often do you make changes . . .? Would you do this if you or your secretary had to type the whole thing out each time?

Thinking

Three minutes though would suffice to find this out, but thought is irksome and three minutes a long time.

A. E. HOUSMAN

- Record ideas. Jot them down as you have them – don't try to remember everything. If you can't write it in your organizer, transfer it as soon as you can. Keep note pads, with pencil attached, about the place so you don't have to hunt for something to write on/with. If you're prone to remembering something in the middle of the night keep one on your bedside table. If you get good ideas while watching television, keep it on the coffee table or by your chair. Use a tape recorder or Dictaphone in the car to record ideas, notes, or use this when you are on the move.
- Have a 'think about' list. Don't consign your 'good ideas' or anything else simply to a note. Notes do you no good unless you remember to think about what you've written. Use waiting time or travelling time to think about issues/problems/projects/what to buy your father for his birthday . . .
- Don't worry before you have to. Panic too soon and everything changes so you end up worrying twice. Don't worry about things you can't do anything about. Balance sensible concern against over-the-top paranoia. No plan is ever 100 per cent certain so don't let worrying about imponderables take up extensive time.

Shopping

- If you can use flexitime to shop at quiet periods do, and don't shop when you know shelves will be empty — usually Monday mornings.
- Shop with a list. Learn the layout of your supermarket and organize your list to match. Plan a route round the shops. Don't keep going backwards and forwards.
- Check by telephone first whether items are in the shops, prices and so forth.
- Distinguish between 'shopping-as-work', that is, shopping with a purpose, when you're out to buy definite things, and 'shopping-as-leisure' or 'window shopping', when you're wandering around, enjoying what you're doing and may or may not buy anything. The two don't always mix terribly well. If you are mixing them, get the 'chore' part over first, otherwise you may never get round to it, or find it hard to make decisions when you do, because you're tired and/or fed-up.

Presents

- Keep an ongoing birthday/Christmas present list. Every time you have an idea, or someone drops a hint about what they might like, make a note of it. Come Christmas half the work is done as thinking about what to buy people has been eliminated.
- Buy all the cards you need for birthdays in one go — this doesn't mean you don't care and don't choose carefully, just that you go through the card racks once instead of several times. Buy a good supply of wrapping paper and tags at the same time.
- When shopping for one present buy for several people at the same time. Again, it eliminates endless trekking round the shops. If you see something that is ideal for someone buy it, even if they've just had a birthday — you'll never find it again.
- If you travel abroad frequently, Christmas or birthday presents from trips show people you were thinking of them while you were away, and you can find something unusual.

- Make one idea do for a number of people at Christmas — particularly family and friends who don't see one another. Or work to a theme. Make this the year that everyone gets ... boxes: everything from hat boxes, jewellery boxes, tool boxes, carved wooden boxes, money boxes, enamelled pill boxes ... help someone get organized and buy them a set of attractive file boxes.
- Keep a notebook/card file with relevant names in it, their date of birth and anniversary dates. That way you don't forget children's ages and important dates. Make a note of each present you buy — then you don't have to worry about repeating what you bought last year or the year before that. If you don't keep a general list note down ideas for future presents.

Waiting and Travelling

You can carry correspondence, bills and similar tasks in your briefcase to do at odd moments, and more substantial work to do on journeys. I confess to never having mastered the art of writing on a moving train (I can, however, sew), so limit the type of work to the situation/your skills. If there is work you can do while waiting or travelling, fine, but don't expect to do your best work, or work that requires a lot of concentration unless you're very good at cutting out distractions. Catching up on reading is a good task for such situations, if it is not something that requires careful analysis. But sometimes why not indulge yourself and not work? Reading a novel you haven't got round to makes good use of second class time and means you arrive more relaxed and ready for business.

PART 3

**Putting
Plans into
Action**

7

PERSONAL PERSPECTIVE ON TIME

Why should we be in such desperate haste to succeed, and in such desperate enterprises? If a man does not keep pace with his companions, perhaps it is because he hears a different drummer.

HENRY DAVID THOREAU

In Chapter 1 you made a list of why you have a time management problem. Let us return to this list. You may have written down 'too much to do' as one reason of many, or the one, global reason. Now you need to think about this. Why do you have too much to do? Write down a list of all the reasons why you think you have too much to do.

Your list will contain some of the ideas below as well as ones of your own:

- I'm given too many jobs/tasks
- I take on too many things — many that aren't my responsibility
- I can't say no
- There is no one to delegate to (literally no one/I don't trust them to do a good job/they're unskilled)
- I'm interested in lots of things
- I have unrealistic time estimates/deadlines
- I enjoy being busy
- I want to look important/busy/successful
- I don't want to miss an opportunity
- My priorities are unclear
- I'm slow, it takes me a long while to do things
- I'm a perfectionist
- I don't want to give anyone else the opportunity
- I need the extra money

Let's say your main answer was 'I can't say no.' Again, ask yourself 'why?' Write down all the reasons. For example:

- I want to be helpful
- I don't want to cause offence
- I don't want to reject someone
- I want to be involved in everything
- Doing things makes me feel important
- If I say no I won't be liked
- I like being busy
- I like to feel needed
- I don't know how to say no with conviction
- Other people don't take no for an answer
- Nice people do things for others

The first thing to learn from this chapter is to keep asking 'why?' Take your main answer from 'I can't say no' and ask 'why?' Imagine you are a young child at the stage when every other word is 'why?' and try to answer yourself. 'Because I say so' doesn't count as an answer (and even your toddler doesn't think much of it either). The aim of this is to try to get at some of the habits in your thinking, your attitudes and beliefs, that contribute to poor time management. As you go through this exercise constantly ask yourself 'why?' You will find that some answers keep getting repeated. Concentrate on these. They are central to your beliefs and your problems. They echo needs such as 'to be needed', 'to be of service', 'to be in control' and 'to know'. In the previous section we concentrated on planning and organizing. If this is working for you, great, but there will inevitably be some bits you know you should do, that you could do, that you would do, if only . . . But somehow you never do. In this section we look at what psychological factors hinder your progress and what you can do about them.

We Are What We Think

Using ideas and techniques from cognitive behaviour therapy and Albert Ellis's rational-emotive therapy you can begin to examine your beliefs and attitudes which contribute to time management problems (and, indeed, other problems as well). All of us have negative thought patterns at some time, but some people get trapped in a negative way of thinking which limits their ability to act or to change. Many of these ideas are current in society, or are patterns of thinking or beliefs you have learnt from your parents or other people important to you, especially when you were a child. Understanding why you have certain beliefs is much less important than understanding what they are, and what maintains them. It is only then you can work actively to change them.

Negative Thought Patterns

All or Nothing Thinking

You think in terms of black and white, ignoring shades of grey. If you can't get total *control*/do something *perfectly*/have *exactly* what you want, you see it as a total failure or not worth bothering. We all know the expression 'a miss is as good as a mile'.

Your excuses for not planning would include:

- If I can't get control of all my time there's no point in trying to control any
- If I can't get rid of this job I don't want to do there's no point in trying to make it easier

You don't say 'I must cut down on unnecessary meetings' but 'I must never go to another useless meeting again.'

By setting all or nothing standards you diminish your ability to change or adapt to a situation; you also discount small steps achieved towards a goal. You need to move from looking at extremes to looking for balance.

Over-generalization

This is similar to all or nothing thinking but it relates to events and abilities. A single negative event becomes proof of general failure on your part. For example, you lose control of one day and don't get everything finished that you planned. Rather than saying 'I can start again tomorrow,' you say 'There's no point in trying, it'll never work, I might as well give up.' Or you miss one deadline and say, 'I'm always late. That's the way I am. I can't do anything about it.'

Labelling

Rather than describing what happened, 'I didn't get my "to do" list finished', you attach labels to yourself: 'I'm useless/inadequate/ awful/a slob/have no will-power'. You may phrase it as a question: 'Why am I so stupid/pathetic/lacking in self-discipline?' When things don't go as you've planned you label yourself worthless.

Should and Ought Statements

You treat yourself like a naughty child being spoken to by a bossy or critical parent. Your conscience says 'I should be able to stick to my time plan' or 'I shouldn't have agreed to go to that meeting when I had the afternoon set aside for prime time work.' You don't ask *why* you should or whether the demands on yourself are realistic, but you probably label yourself negatively when you don't do what you think you should.

Should often occurs in conjunction with self-discipline. What is 'self-discipline'?

Fortune Telling

You're so convinced that things will turn out badly that you act as though they already have done so. The future is a fact you have predicted and you intend to make sure it happens:

- 'I'm going to fail at planning . . .', so you don't do it properly
- 'I'll never have enough time . . .', so you don't start
- 'It's impossible to plan because there are so many emergencies . . .', so you don't try anything

Ignoring the Positive

You ignore what you have done and concentrate on what you haven't or what went wrong, or you don't even notice the nice things that happen to you, but concentrate on the bad/nasty things: 'I got *A* finished this week but so what? It should have been finished weeks ago/I should have done *B* as well/and as for *C* . . . it's not even started.'

Catastrophizing

This rather ugly word means that when things don't go the way you want them to you respond by saying 'It's awful/terrible/the end of the world'. You always jump to the worst conclusion. Some things are awful, but most of what we label 'awful' is disappointing/sad/a pity/regretful/a minor irritation/a nuisance but not out-and-out awful. A minor upset gets defined as a crisis. Take a tip from Winston Churchill who used to take a nap every day with the instruction that he was to be woken only in the event of a crisis; he then added that by crisis he meant 'the armed invasion of the British Isles'. You predict disasters so you don't act: 'If I tell my boss I can't take any more work on he'll be angry and I'll lose my job.' How likely, realistically, is that?

You may not catastrophize in terms of disasters, but you respond like a child: 'It's not fair!' Maybe it isn't, but that doesn't change things. It often ties in with believing that good things happen (particularly to other people) because of luck and not effort.

'Yes . . . But'

Someone offers you a suggestion or solution to a problem. You see a flaw: 'Yes . . . but ..' Another solution, another flaw: 'Yes . . .

but ...' Sometimes the situation is complex and you are raising
genuine objections which can be ironed out. Often you are making
excuses, rationalizing why you don't intend to do anything about
changing. Once you hear yourself say 'Yes . . . but . . .' for the third
time stop and ask yourself whether you really want to change, or
whether you're simply paying lip service to the notion.

Alternative Thoughts

If you are going to change successfully you need to replace these
negative thought habits with more positive ones. This can be achieved
by a two-pronged approach.

Examine the Facts

Be realistic in your assessment of consequences. Was it really a
mistake of epic proportions which has far-reaching consequences for
you/your family/the company/the universe as we know it, or was it
a minor blunder which has been successfully contained?

When things have not gone as well as you hoped, consider whether
you were being over-optimistic? Remind yourself what you have done
successfully in the past. Give yourself an A for effort — you tried; with
practice you will improve.

Find More Realistic Thoughts

The negative thoughts will keep returning unless you replace them
with something. Having examined the facts you can use this to
introduce new, realistic thoughts:

- 'One slip isn't the end of the world'
- 'I might have had a bad day but I've done well for two weeks
  and no one's perfect'
- 'At least I tried and I don't have to go through life wondering
  "what if . . ."'

Fall back on clichés if necessary while you develop your own realistic ideas. Use anything that seems appropriate from 'If at first you don't succeed, try, try, try again' or 'It's better to have loved and lost than never loved at all' to 'Faint heart ne'er won fair lady'.

Problem Beliefs

There are some beliefs we hold and assumptions we make which contribute to our inability to manage time. As you debate these issues with yourself (or with others) keep asking why? The more you push yourself to give reasons, and the harder it gets, the more you will be able to recognize how absurd some of them are.

Doing Something Useful

In Chapter 1, I asked you to think about your approach to work, whether you are a workaholic. Why do you always need to be busy? Do you really believe the devil will find work for your idle hands? Do you feel guilty about enjoying yourself? Why? Do you justify pleasures by doing something useful: 'It's all right to watch *Dallas* because I'm cleaning the oven at the same time'? The useful activity justifies the fun.

Success Is . . .

Success is . . . always being busy/not having a moment to yourself/not having time to go on holiday . . . Is this really success? How else might you define it? What about the luxury of time to spend with your family? by yourself? Does your definition of success push you into taking on more than you can sensibly deal with?

I Need to Know

The need to know is admirable if it is a curiosity which encourages research, questioning, innovation and invention. Unfortunately, all too often the 'need to know' is motivated by nothing more than not wanting to be left out. It can also be used as an excuse not to act: 'I can't make this decision until I know . . .', 'I'll write this article when I've read more . . .' Such inaction and absence of a quest for knowledge can be motivated by the need for reassurance (that you're not going to make the wrong decision) or that somewhere there is the one, right, perfect answer. Information overload is a major problem for many of us, contributing to our work load, storage problems and general feeling of not-being-on-top-of-things, not being up-to-date (see Chapter 11).

It's Fate

Another 'good' excuse for inaction. Do you honestly believe that things happen because they are fated, or simply because of luck or chance? A variation on this is 'when the time is right . . .' It usually means never.

I Can Do It Better/Faster Myself

This is used as a reason not to delegate (see Chapter 10). In the short term this is sometimes true, but does nothing to solve the long-term problem. If you have staff you don't trust to do the work is it because they're not competent/skilled, or that they wouldn't do it 'properly' (i.e. exactly as you would)? If it is the former, get them trained to do the job. If it is the latter ask yourself whether they are doing the job appropriately/competently. If so, what is the problem? If you simply don't trust them, is this based on something real, or on your own prejudices and need for reassurance?

If you're saying 'I don't have time to explain/show them', incorporate this training into your goals and planning, and save yourself time in the long run. When our children are young and learning to dress themselves it slows down getting out of the house in the morning considerably, but we persevere, because we want them to have the skill of dressing themselves and also because *we* don't want to be buttoning them into their coats when they're 18.

Perfectionism

> *Our life is frittered away by detail ... simplify, simplify.*
> HENRY DAVID THOREAU

'I'm a perfectionist.' This is often said in a tone of smug self-congratulation. Who, after all, can criticize you for wanting things done well. It becomes a problem when it is combined with an all-or-nothing approach. *Everything* has to be done well. Ask yourself why. What would happen if something was done only adequately? If you want everything you do to be done really well, as near to perfect as you can make it, you are likely to be getting very uncomfortable with the idea that some things need not be perfect. Why? I'm not saying everything has to be adequate or that this always means second best, or second rate. Some things should always be done as well as you can possibly do them – I want aeroplanes that stay up, trains that stay on rails, buildings that are weatherproof and I don't want second-rate surgery any more than anyone else.

What we are talking about is standards and this only makes sense if you take into account consequences, time available, effort needed, resources and who else is involved. I am suggesting you apply a cost-benefit analysis and make judgements about standards based on that. Is it better to do something as well as you can in the time available and meet the deadline, or do it better than that (more perfectly) and miss the deadline? Is it better to re-write one letter half a dozen times until it is as polished as you can make it, and not do the other five, or write six adequate letters? Inevitably the answer will partly depend on who it is going to. When you are putting all this effort into your letter, however, bear in mind that in business people only read quickly through letters once, they will probably miss the subtlety of your prose in their haste to understand the gist of what you have to say.

Modifying standards is not about doing everything poorly, or becoming a slob. It is about being *appropriate*. Sometimes perfectionism is worth striving for. Sterilizing equipment for surgery is one thing but your kitchen can be hygienic without it doubling as an operating theatre.

Even the most dedicated perfectionist makes standard judgements all the time, even if they don't realize they're doing it. Each day you, or someone in your family, produces a meal. Are they always the same standard? You make a decision based on resources – the money you want to spend, the time you have available – and outcome measures, including who will eat the meal: is it just your family or is the boss or your in-laws who are coming? You make a judgement that, given a crude cost-benefit analysis, tonight it is beans-on-toast or a four-course cordon bleu banquet. *This* is setting appropriate standards.

The two basic questions you need to ask yourself are: 'Will my striving for perfection improve something that is worth improving?' and 'Does my perfectionism stop me doing things?' This can be either because one thing takes so long you have no time for anything else, or it can stop you acting at all because you fear you won't achieve your impossibly high standards.

There is an old children's saying:

> *Good, better, best,*
> *Never let it rest,*
> *Until the good is better*
> *And the better best.*

This is a noble sentiment when it encourages you to improve a skill, develop an idea, refine a design. It is a problem when 'the good' is not achieved (because you never start) because you fear you will never achieve 'the best'.

If perfectionism is stopping you doing things, or eating into your time, you need to ask yourself what drives your need to be perfect. Are you repeating another childhood saying: 'If a thing's worth doing it's worth doing well.' Why? Have you converted 'well' into 'as "well" as I can possibly do it'. Why? Try out the idea that some things are worth doing adequately. This usually means 'well' within given limits of time, resources, energy, priority and interest.

Maybe you think you'll only gain approval if you do something perfectly? Or it will make people like you (more)? Is this true? Are these reasonable, rational beliefs?

In one workshop a minister said that he had been brought up to believe that you should do everything perfectly because everything we do we do to the glory of God. If this is a sincerely held belief, reflected in every aspect of your life, it is a way of life which goes beyond managing your time. For most of us it is not. The Shakers strove for perfection because part of their belief is the possibility of perfection here and now. Life progresses from one accomplishment to another. They developed many labour-saving devices ranging from the automatic washing machine to the circular saw and the apple corer, but the reason for this was so they were able to limit their time working and increase their time in prayer and worship. Their striving for perfectionism resulted in simplification and elimination of detail in every aspect of their life, not in rewriting a letter for the sixth time.

Lastly, ask yourself what you mean by perfect. What is the perfect letter? Can a letter be perfect? The meaning can be clear or confused, its purpose can be straightforward or ambiguous, it can be typed with errors or without mistakes, the layout can be pleasing and elegant, or untidy and cramped ... but perfect?

If you still want to stick to being a 'perfectionist' consider the advice: 'If thou wilt be perfect, go and sell that thou hast, and give to the poor, and thou shalt have treasure in heaven' (Matthew 19.21). Is this what you mean by perfect?

Procrastination

Procrastination is the thief of time.
EDWARD YOUNG

It is a rare person who never prevaricates, who never puts things off. Although we all know someone (maybe ourself) who is an habitual procrastinator most of us only procrastinate in certain areas. Dedicated procrastinators put their life on hold — 'I'll do it (or worse, think about it) when I'm 30/when I've lost weight/when I've got my inheritance/when the children have left home/when I retire ..'

Whether you always procrastinate or whether it is a rare occurrence the cycle is always the same.

Cycle of Procrastination

J. B. Burka and L. M. Yeun describe the cycle of procrastination which we all recognize:

- 'This time I'll make an early start' . . . you're hopeful, optimistic, *but* 'I can't start right now . . .'
- 'I must start soon' . . . you begin to feel twinges of anxiety, but are still fairly hopeful as the deadline is some way off
- 'Suppose I never start' . . . your anxiety is getting stronger as you imagine dire consequences of never starting. A variety of responses can now occur:
  - Guilt:

    'I should have started sooner'

    'I shouldn't be doing/enjoying this' (when you're taking time off)

  - Distraction:

    'I'm doing *something*' (even if it has nothing to do with the task)

    You can even convince yourself that what you're doing is moving the task forward: 'If I tidy my desk I'll have more space to work'

  - Shame:

    'What will people think if they find out?' You may hide the fact that no progress is being made with a variety of creative deceptions: the dog got hold of the floppy disc/my young son threw his cereal all over it . . .

    You either try to look busy or literally hide

- 'I can still do it' . . . you're desperately hanging on to this belief, hoping to dispel your negative feelings as you wait for the task to spontaneously start

- 'What's wrong with me?' . . . to take your mind off the anxiety of not completing the task and the possible consequences, you move to an even bigger worry: that something is wrong with you that you can't get on with the task
- 'It's now or never' . . . It's the final crunch: time and your ability to tolerate anxiety and worry have run out:
  - Never . . . you give up. Doing the task in the time that is left is impossible so you see no other choice. You either say 'I can't do it now' or 'why bother?' You confirm your own feeling of inadequacy.
  - Now! Everything has become so intolerable that getting on with the task is better than putting it off any longer. It's usually accompanied by feelings of 'It's not as bad as I expected' and a hyped-up feeling of 'challenge' or 'excitement' as you rush to beat the deadline.
- 'I'll never procrastinate again' . . . is the promise made in the heat of euphoria, relief and exhaustion at having finished, or in the depths of despondency at giving up
- 'This time I'll make an early start' . . . but not right now

Without a plan you've learnt nothing and have no way of changing your behaviour.

If all this sounds familiar to you you've been guilty of procrastination at some time.

What Do You Procrastinate Over?

Write out a list of the tasks you put off doing, including tasks from your home and personal life as well as work. We want to examine why you procrastinate and it will be helpful to know whether different situations produce the same or different kinds of problems.

Now write down a list of the things you say to yourself when you're putting something off. We will come back to examine these lists shortly.

Conditions For Procrastination

For procrastination to grow and flourish there are two optimal conditions, usually occurring together:

Scarlett O'Hara Syndrome

Like the heroine of *Gone With the Wind* you take tomorrow as your watchword. You don't have to do it now because there is time in the future when you can do the task – it doesn't matter that the time is illusory, or too short, or too distant. The future is a fantasy land of completed tasks and fulfilled ambitions, truly a Never-Never Land. This is a particular problem for people in jobs which are fairly open-ended, and/or who are happy to work evenings and weekends. In such cases it is easy to say 'I'll do it later'. Stock markets closing/planting in the spring/a deal going to someone else can force deadlines on you.

Hedonism

There is something more pleasurable to do now. It may not, in the normal run of things, be pleasurable at all, but compared to the task you are putting off – filing/clearing your desk/washing the floor/weeding/answering your correspondence – it seems positively pleasurable.

Procrastination is about putting pleasure before pain. Overcoming procrastination means confronting why tasks are painful.

Why Do You Procrastinate?

> *There is no expedient to which a man will not resort to avoid the real labour of thinking.*
>
> SIR JOSHUA REYNOLDS

Using the categories below go over your list of tasks you put off, assigning a reason to each of them. The list of reasons, covert and overt, that procrastinators use below also helps. Compare this with your list of reasons and see where you need to amend it. Strategies for overcoming procrastination will not be effective unless you deal with the underlying reasons.

I must be perfect
If a thing's worth doing it's worth doing well
The risk is too great
I can't risk failure
If I win someone will lose
Why should I make the effort?
If I do it well this time I'll always have to do it (well)
I can't let go
Why should I do what someone else wants?
Rules are for other people
I don't want to face a challenge
I must do everything well
Things should go easily and require little effort
Challenge is another word for risk/problem
If I give in to them I'll lose myself
I want them to be nice to me so I'll do it
There is ONE, RIGHT answer and I'll wait until I've found it

What Procrastinators Say

It Might Go Away

You may put off doing something because past experience has taught you that not doing it won't matter, or the person giving it to you will change their mind or forget it altogether. This is not procrastination, but a deliberate, sensible decision. Neither is it procrastination when you are genuinely waiting for further details. It is procrastination when you only hope something will go away. Occasionally you get lucky, but remember that luck is nothing more than random factors operating in your favour. Next time they might go against you. And some things, no matter how much you hope, you know won't go away.

Nasty Tasks

Many of the things we put off doing come into the 'nasty' category. They are the things that are either boring or unpleasant, ranging from filling in your tax forms/making an appointment with the dentist/disciplining someone/telephoning someone who you think will be difficult/dealing with a complaint/doing the ironing . . .

Sometimes a 'nasty' task can be difficult or dangerous. This in itself can be reason enough to put it off, but it may have more to do with the next category: fear of failing. When it doesn't, the task is probably bigger and more complex than you thought. It's difficult because you don't have the right skills and you don't want to take the time or can't be bothered to learn them, or you realize that it involves much bigger changes than you had anticipated – learning time management means more than clearing your desk and buying a Filofax.

Fear of Failing

You might be uncertain of your competence to do the task, or the required standards are unclear. Rather than learn the necessary skills or seek clarification, you choose the apparently easier option of procrastination.

Procrastination means we don't have to face our fears and that is a useful strategy for minimizing anxiety (i.e. the worry over procrastination is less than the anxiety over risking failure). One good example of this is the person who leaves something to the last minute, but can just get it done. Listen to yourself (or someone else) saying 'It would have been better if I'd had more time.' In fact, you did have more time, you just didn't use it. Procrastination protects you from saying 'this is the best I can do' and then somebody saying 'it's not good enough'. By leaving things until the last minute you always have an excuse to counteract criticism: 'I didn't have any more time.' This is often the 'get-out' for the perfectionist.

Fear of Succeeding

It's easy to understand fear of failing, but what about fear of succeeding? It might tie in with a nasty task, and your concern is that if you do it well you end up having to do it again. Understandable, but procrastination is not the answer. Being assertive is. Either say no, or do it and say no next time (see Chapter 10).

By succeeding you may be concerned that more will be expected of you – either to keep doing the task well, or to do other things. The former might hide a fear of failing ('I did it well once but I'm not sure I can do it well every time'). The latter might tie in with not wanting to do something forever, or fearing that your lifestyle will change in a way that you don't want it to. This is reflected in 'If I succeed I'll change', or 'Other people will treat me differently', or 'They will be envious of me/won't like me'. All these are seen as negative results of succeeding, so not trying is easier, more pleasant.

You may be afraid of exposing yourself by expressing an interest in winning/succeeding or even trying. Procrastination hides your ambition. This may be a particular problem for women who have been culturally conditioned to be supportive of others rather than to succeed on their own behalf.

Some people see succeeding themselves as diminishing someone else. Your promotion means bad news for a colleague. Again women are more prone to this – their procrastination means their career doesn't move faster than their husband's. People with low self-esteem may shun success because 'I don't deserve it' and may even worry that they will be punished for it.

For each of these you need to confront your fears and ask how rational they are. Is it worth the risk? What can you do to minimize risk?

Control

Although procrastination often feels like being out of control you can use it to gain control in hidden ways. You've been asked, or worse, told, to do something which isn't your choice. By procrastinating you exercise what little control you have: 'He told me to do it now – I'll do it later'; 'She wants this done today, I'll start tomorrow'. Sometimes you put something off simply *because* you've been told to do it, without even thinking about it. You get a message to telephone someone between 2 p.m. and 3 p.m. There's no reason why you can't. You even want to speak to them. But you leave it until 3.10 p.m., just to exert your independence/authority/control, and then wonder why they're not there.

You can use procrastination to show your annoyance with someone — you put off doing what they want, even if it has nothing to do with why you're annoyed; or to show that you are more powerful than they are/to make them beholden to you when you do get around to doing it/to make them humble themselves to ask or beg you/to get back at someone . . . At its most extreme, thwarting the other person ('the enemy') becomes more important than doing what you want.

There are numerous ways you might want to control someone, and even more reasons why.

Defence

In a world full of uncertainty and unpredictability procrastination means that you put off committing yourself — to an idea, a project, a person — and this, you believe, minimizes your risk of being hurt. Procrastination as a form of defence is common in relationships; you don't have to reveal your needs/weaknesses/dependency if you're waiting for the other person to reveal theirs first. It often goes with the need to control; you see co-operating with others, 'the enemy', as giving up your independence.

Closeness With Others

You can use procrastination either directly or indirectly to manipulate your relationships with others. If you are in a comfortable, dependent relationship you may prefer to maintain this rather than branching out on your own. You can try to achieve closeness with others by procrastinating over something so long that you can no longer do it on your own — you have to ask others for help, or they will feel bound to help you. You can also use it to gain sympathy when you look so tired and stressed as you struggle to do everything. You can procrastinate over a job change because you don't want to leave someone — a boy/girlfriend might seem reasonable — but a boss? colleagues?

Closeness can be achieved not just with people, but with things. Hoarding is procrastinating about throwing things away and means you're never alone, never without — you keep everything 'just-in-case'. Consider whether you are holding on to something not because 'it might be useful' but rather 'in case I feel lost without it'.

As well as using procrastination to develop ties, you can use it to maintain distance, which might overlap with being defensive. You agree to meet someone for lunch — but never get round to setting a date. Or it might be that you feel other people, by getting too close, will take something away from you. By persisting in this belief you can loose sight of your own real needs, wishes and interests.

Overcoming Procrastination

Most of the techniques for overcoming procrastination work well with the dull, boring, difficult and generally nasty tasks. They also have reasonable success with milder forms of the other reasons for procrastination. For habitual procrastinators who put off living, and for some of the deep-seated psychological reasons why you procrastinate, you will need more detailed advice than there is room for here or you may even need counselling or therapy.

Feel Virtuous

We've all done this on occasions — basked in a golden halo of smug virtue when we've done something we didn't like, didn't have to (but altruistically have) or finished something ahead of time. It's a very nice feeling (although it can antagonize others) and is worth remembering as a reward for not putting things off.

Some people choose their nastiest task and start the day with that, on the grounds that the day can only get better. They feel good from the sense of achievement and this pushes them on to the next task with increased enthusiasm. If control is important to you then polishing off an unpleasant task proves that you're in control of it, not that it is controlling you. A warm glow of smugness will accompany this.

Do It

Just as it is going into a cold swimming pool, tackling things you don't like doing slowly is much more painful. Jump in and get the shock over with quickly! The longer you leave something the bigger it gets – psychologically if not in actuality. Every time you move your tax forms you're reminded that you still haven't done them. You feel guilty. This goes on until the feelings of guilt and awfulness of the task are far in excess of the task itself.

Make a start, even if you can't do the whole task at one go. This usually confirms that it's not as bad as you thought it was going to be and returning to it is less difficult.

Plan It

Put it in your diary and then do it (as above). Routine tasks that you habitually prevaricate over can be incorporated into your schedule so that you never have to think about doing them – it has become automatic. Reducing the number of decisions you have to make about doing a task minimizes the number of times you can put it off. Pick a time you can be reasonably sure you'll always be able to use. Our grandmothers did this unquestioningly: Monday *was* washday. Who argued?

Little and Often

Break a task up into manageable chunks and do it a piece at a time. Unless you're feeling masochistic don't try and do one big, nasty thing all in one go (unless there is absolutely no option) and don't group nasty tasks together. Anyone with sense and a degree of self-preservation is more likely to avoid a day of misery than just half an hour. If the tasks require effort and thought you're more likely to make mistakes as you go from one task to the next, resenting each one. Integrate things that are boring with tasks that are interesting, the unpleasant with the pleasant, the difficult with the easy. Changing pace throughout the day will help prevent fatigue and boredom.

It usually helps to leave a task at a place where it easy to pick up again rather than when you've reached a problem. Knowing you've to return to a mess makes it harder. Sometimes, however, problems have a way of resolving themselves while you're doing something else. This is particularly true if you're working past your point of being efficient. If you're writing something and get stuck, or can't get started again, rewrite the last page to get you into the flow again and very often you'll be able to continue without undue effort.

Think Positively

You've already tried virtue, but add to it. Stop listening to all the negative, distracting things you're saying — it's hard/it's not fair/why should I have to do it?/I don't like this . . . If you keep telling yourself doing something is awful how can it possibly be anything else? Try to imagine doing the task with pleasure and if this is difficult at least concentrate on how good you will feel when it's done — the sense of relief and achievement, the weight being lifted from your shoulders. Remind yourself that it is not as bad as it seems. Past experience usually supports this, and even if it is as bad as it seems you can still anticipate having it finished.

Use Reinforcement

Earlier I pointed out that procrastination is about pleasure before pain; remind yourself that pleasure can be better after pain. If you've been feeling guilty and can't enjoy going out because of some chore left undone, think how much more you'll enjoy it, free of guilt, when the task is completed. Plan rewards for yourself – time off/a cup of coffee/a more interesting task/a chat with a friend ... Make the reward commensurate with the effort involved in the task and don't cheat! It might sound a bit childish, but we all do it much of the time without thinking about it. Try when I've washed the kitchen floor/ typed this report/mowed the lawn/finished the budget/written this chapter-sermon-article-report-shopping list then I'll put my feet up for half an hour/have a drink/telephone x/watch *Neighbours* ...

Get Help

If you can afford it you can always pay someone to do it for you, be it the housework/writing a speech/filling in your tax returns/being on call at night ... If it is appropriate to delegate (see Chapter 10) do so, otherwise swap your skills if you really don't want/need to learn how to do it. Your nasty task isn't necessarily someone else's nasty task and you may be able to exchange chores with colleagues, friends or family members. A department or family discussion can throw up some surprising findings. Something you've always considered a bore and a chore may be seen by a colleague as a challenge. If all else fails, share the task, returning the favour. Shared boredom (or misery) provides a distraction which eases the pain. A dull task completed with a friend can become fun, and you can return the help. Somehow cleaning someone else's house/garden/garage is never as bad as doing your own.

Use Deadlines Positively

Set realistic deadlines for each part of the task. If self-imposed deadlines don't work well for you, use rewards to make them stick. Or don't allow yourself to take on a new, interesting piece of work without finishing one of the tasks hanging over you. If appropriate, announce deadlines to family, friends or colleagues. Queries as to how a project is coming on may push you into action. Contrive to find external deadlines – a conference at which to present a paper makes you deal with data and, equally, a committee meeting can force you to formulate your ideas/collect your thoughts together so you can present them coherently. Holidays can provide a real incentive to clear your desk of outstanding tasks. Things that you have happily left lying for weeks seem urgent when you're going to be away for a fortnight. If necessary, take more holidays.

Novel Solutions

Take a tip from Luke Rhinehart's novel, *The Dice Man*. List six activities or chores, some nice, some nasty, or some easy, some challenging (ignore, as he doesn't, some illegal, some immoral) and then roll the dice to determine which you will do next.

Bernice Rubens's novel *A Five Year Sentence* has an elderly spinster in it who writes up her day in her diary the day *before*, thus compelling her to do it to ensure that she has written the truth.

Change Cultures

If all else fails, move to a place which values the slow pace of life.

A story is told of an American tracing his ancestors in the Western Isles of Scotland and being frustrated by the slowness with which things happened. He commented on this to a local and asked what the Gaelic equivalent of *mañana* was. The local pondered for a while before replying, then said: 'We don't have a word that conveys quite that sense of urgency.'

8

PUTTING PLANS INTO ACTION

The philosophers have only interpreted the world in various ways: the point is to change it.

KARL MARX

You probably started this book full of good intentions about changing your behaviour – quickly and easily. You may have already started to change some of your habits and challenge some of your beliefs. But all of us have, at varying times, made good resolutions, changing for a while and then slipping back into old habits. This may be because of negative consequences we hadn't even thought about, including pressure from others, or simply the strength of the habit. Planning comes first, but often change gets no further than plans. Putting the plans into action is the next stage. Having done this we realize that it is not the changing of behaviour that is the most difficult, or important, but the maintenance of that change.

This chapter looks at creating and maintaining change for two reasons. Firstly, so that you can apply these principles to changing your time management related behaviour, and secondly, so that you can apply them to changing other behaviour. To keep trying to change something and failing is not only demoralizing, it is a waste of time.

Some areas of change will be easier than others, and one object of this chapter is to point out areas of 'sabotage' that you might not have considered. These should be examined when you can't get past the planning stage or when repeated attempts to change fail. Previous knowledge of them should help the change process to go more smoothly.

Do You Really Need to Change?

Difficulties in getting started, or moving from planning to action, can relate to how you view the 'problem'. Rather than simply accept that you 'have to do something about it', consider how much you really need to change.

How Much of a Problem Have You Got?

Rather than thinking globally about your problem, look at it in bits. In some situations you can manage your time. When? Why? What can you learn from this? What bits of your behaviour are a problem? Stop thinking in an all or none fashion.

Try to quantify the problem, and set measurable goals.

What Are the Risks of Your Behaviour?

If you don't change and keep going exactly as you are what will happen to your health/happiness/satisfaction/relationships/economic stability/reputation/ . . .?

Why Do You Want to Change?

In other words, what is your motivation? Does it come from yourself, or from other people? Pressure from other people to change is rarely as powerful as self-motivation unless they exert enormous control over you and have powerful sanctions. If the pressure comes from others consider:

- How worthy are the other person's motives?
- Does it point to a problem in your relationship?
- *Whose* problem is it?
- What will happen if you don't change/comply with their wishes?

Are There Advantages to Staying as You Are?

What are the pay-offs from your 'problem'? These will be discussed later. It doesn't mean that you shouldn't change, but it does mean you have to examine these consequences and plan how you will handle them.

Do You Really Want to Change?

Really wanting to change means more than motivation, it also involves considering, and closing, the gap between what you want to achieve and what is realistic; the difference between ambition and reality.

Ability and Resources

> *When we mean to build,*
> *We first survey the plot, then draw the model:*
> *And when we see the figure of the house,*
> *Then we must rate the cost of the erection:*
> *Which if we find outweighs ability,*
> *What do we then but draw anew the model*
> *In fewer offices, or at last desist*
> *To build at all?*

WILLIAM SHAKESPEARE

Although we may speak of ability to pay and internal or psychological resources, it is probably easiest for now to think of ability as personal attributes and resources as externals upon which you can draw.

Realistically recognising your abilities, both your strengths and your weaknesses, is a positive aspect of the change process which occasionally has limiting consequences. If you accept a weakness on your part you may automatically dismiss opportunities or ways of doing things. If you keep telling yourself 'I'm numerically illiterate',

'I have no sense of direction' or 'I'm no good at planning' this description becomes part of you and you will unknowingly seek to perpetuate it because it is psychologically comfortable. By the same token, if you only play on your strengths you may miss out on all kinds of opportunities or experiences you don't know whether you'll be good at until you try. Sticking with what you know you can do can easily lead to stagnation.

If you have no resources in one area then it helps to have them in another if you are to succeed in changing. You can't save time like you can money, to spend when you need it, but having money may 'save time' if you use it to buy help. You can give up certain things altogether – by paying someone to do your housework/the gardening/look after your children ... You can have things done more efficiently and/or effectively by paying for particular talents – your dinner parties catered for/your speeches written/your house interior designed ... You can pay to short cut a process – taking a taxi rather than public transport and/or walking, flying rather than train/car ... You can pay for lessons/advice which speed up/improve the learning process – everything from public speaking to computing. Lastly, you can pay for motivation – personal trainers who make sure you exercise and diet counsellors who stop you eating. Going on a course provides enthusiasm and, because you've gone public, may shame you into (at least temporary) change.

Having no money is very time consuming.

Opportunity

I am a great believer in luck, and I find the harder I work the more I have of it.

THOMAS JEFFERSON

So much is written about assertiveness and people's difficulties in saying 'no' that we rarely stop to consider that saying 'yes' to things can also be difficult. Although you may believe having too much to do is part of your time management problem, it may also be a way of protecting yourself from exploring new areas or ideas. You've stuck with what is safe, albeit rather too much of it. Opportunities, chance, luck, call it what you will, cannot be supplied to order, and although chance plays a part you can help the process. You are less likely to be in 'the right place at the right time' if you never go anywhere. Issues to consider in saying yes and saying no are outlined in Chapter 3.

Discipline

Punishment is only one of the meanings of discipline but it is the one we most often think of when we talk about self-discipline – and usually along with the idea of will-power. These are not the most helpful concepts when we're thinking of changing our behaviour, having as they do connotations of moral self-righteousness: if you can't do something it is because you're weak-willed, have no self-discipline, and are a generally unworthy person.

It is better to concentrate on the primary meaning of discipline as learning or instruction. It then becomes a positive commitment to learning, training or following a course. Think disciple.

Commitment

How much do you want something? What are you prepared to do to get it? What are you prepared to give up? You need to make a cost-benefit analysis of the effort involved in change set against the benefits. You need to be enthusiastic about your proposed course of action as second-hand enthusiasm won't carry you very far.

Creating Change – The Problems

Bound by Old Habits

Change is not easy although we usually assume it should be. We are bound by old habits and overestimate our capacity to change. Changing the habits of a lifetime, whether of behaviour or thought, does not happen overnight. Sometimes changing a small problem can be harder than changing a big one. This is because any change requires motivation, time, energy, effort and commitment and this input can appear to be greater than the perceived impact of a small change. When we start the change process we are not usually aware of all the ramifications of both the problem behaviour and its replacement. We find ourselves involved in something bigger than we had expected and suddenly the effort seems too much trouble. At this point, it is easier to slink back into our safe, comfortable rut than to try to pull ourselves out of it.

We give up the change process as our attempts at self-improvement seem to end up confirming how inadequate we really are when we make the same mistakes over and over again. The way out of this maze is to remember that we are aiming for a healthier or happier life and that success is finding the right way forward for ourselves, to suit our personality, beliefs and situation. It also means persevering and not giving up at the first set-back or when things become hard. Whether you take Robert the Bruce's spider or Thomas the 'I think I can' Tank Engine as your role model the message is to keep trying.

Illogical Connections

People often make glib connections between one event and another, or between outward appearance and inner state. It can get interpreted as an over-generalization of anyone who has a problem in one area (e.g. they smoke)/has no self control/no self-discipline/are generally weak. This is manifestly not true. People can have what others (or even themselves) perceive to be a problem in one area and be eminently successful elsewhere.

Because you don't manage your time well doesn't mean you are generally a slob/ineffectual/hopeless. Don't judge yourself (or others) simply by one or two traits/instances and generalize from them. Neither should you assume that what works for one person (even the majority) has to work for you. Both Mozart and Einstein worked in a mess. People who are wedded to 'a cluttered desk is the sign . . .' will say they could have done more if they'd tidied up. How do they know? Maybe they would have done less.

There is one cautionary note here, where a problem in one area will spill over and influence all others, and that is substance abuse. If you have a serious alcohol or drug problem then almost certainly your whole life will be out of control. Other addictive behaviours such as compulsive gambling or compulsive shopping/spending also have far-reaching effects.

Temporary Solutions

This is summed up by the person who says 'If only I could get the backlog cleared up I'd be OK.' The assumption is that the backlog is the problem and all you need to do is get rid of it without any need to look at what caused it in the first place. Even if it magically disappeared you'd have a problem again within a few weeks. You need to tackle the roots of the problem, not tidy up the fallen leaves.

Getting control of your time doesn't mean sorting out priorities and plans so that in a couple of months you can go back to your old ways.

Knowledge Isn't Behaviour

Behaviour does not necessarily follow attitudes. We all know people who believe smoking damages their health yet continue to smoke, or people who say they are not chauvinist/racist/mean/humourless/ vain/vindictive . . . and yet their behaviour proclaims these very traits. Knowing what you have to do doesn't mean that you can do it. It is often easier to become introspective about why you have a problem than to do something about it, particularly if you can find someone to blame: 'I can't help it, it's the way I was brought up.'

Knowledge can help change behaviour, but it isn't the whole answer.

Availability of Behaviour

Knowing the principles of rock climbing doesn't mean you're ready to scale the Matterhorn. Knowing the principles of time management doesn't mean you can immediately put them to use, it takes practice and feedback. You might know how to use your diary to block time in theory, but putting this into practice requires motivation, assertiveness, the ability to stick to your decisions or priorities and a certain amount of co-operation from others.

There is a lot to be said for trying to change behaviour, that is, replacing old habits with new ones, without worrying too much about attitudes/beliefs in the first instance, and only investigating these in stubborn areas. Changing your image of yourself takes time and you will be using many time management techniques successfully for quite a while before you stop thinking of yourself as hopelessly out of control or a poor time manager.

Unrealistic Expectations

The underlying irrational beliefs and unrealistic explanations that support problem behaviour are discussed in detail in Chapter 7. While you're thinking about change globally you should consider your unrealistic expectations regarding:

- How much you can change
- How fast you can change
- How much (or how little) effort is required
- What the outcome will be

If you have unrealistic expectations about the impact of managing your time, for yourself or for others, then no matter what progress you make, what you achieve, it will never seem enough. And you might be tempted to give up on it. Realistically you can aim for outcomes such as feeling more in control/moving ahead on what is important to you (specific goals)/achieving more/working less/having more time with your family/feeling less tired, stressed, harassed . . .

Getting control of your time may give you more time to socialize, but if you don't have any friends it won't provide any. It may give you time with your family, but won't solve the marital problems that caused you to work long hours in the first place. If you're boring because you're a workaholic, working less won't automatically make you more interesting. These are separate problems which require their own solutions.

The Means Become the End

The process of change can take over. Rather than using time management principles to give you time to enjoy what you want to do, saving seconds becomes a way of life. And a limiting way of life at that. Planning takes over so that instead of using it to work on your priorities, having a daily plan (no matter how unimportant the tasks) becomes the objective. Every second becomes accounted for so that there is no time for spontaneity, chance, the random elements of life. Having a clear desk becomes the objective, so everything gets thrust out of sight in a hopeless jumble.

Time management is a means to an end, not an end in itself.

The Impact of Change on Other People

Other people may not want you to change. Their life may be easier if you stay as you are. The reason for this and their techniques for applying pressure are discussed in Chapter 10.

Creating Change – The Alternatives to Will-Power

Will-power all too often becomes won't-power: 'I won't take on more work'; 'I won't smoke that cigarette'; 'I won't eat that cake.' But we do. So if will-power doesn't work what does?

Reinforcement

The satisfaction you get when you make a change in your habits only goes so far and wears a bit thin before your new behaviour has firmly established itself. This is the time you need to make use of rewards to keep you going until habit once more takes over. Use whatever is available to/suitable for to you and your circumstances. Make it appropriate to the effort involved – no big treats for small achievements. You don't have to send yourself into bankruptcy to do this; rewards don't have to be material, but can be social or personal. Anything counts: having coffee with or without a friend/watching a favourite television programme/working on something you really enjoy/reading a novel/having extra time with your children/putting your feet up and doing absolutely nothing . . .

Your reward might be something as simple, and as hard, as praising yourself. If you're always negative towards yourself this is an important step forward. And don't give yourself half-hearted rewards: no 'you did a good job but it would have been better if . . .' Stop before you get to the *but* or all you'll hear is the *but*. Analyse what you could learn from it later and how it could (possibly) be improved, but enjoy the achievement first.

Reinforcement only works if you don't cheat – and if you do, the only person you're cheating is yourself.

Feedback

Learn from what you do. Feedback is about knowledge of results. You can only improve if you measure what you do against some standard.

You'll never learn to play darts if you don't see where they land. You won't see progress if you don't have a baseline and a goal. Why did something go well? Badly? How can you prevent it happening again? Ask other people for their views to get different opinions and to put your own into perspective.

Be Consistent in Your Response

Whether the new behaviour involves only you or other people if you give in and retreat to your previous response, you only make it harder next time. If you're resisting taking on a piece of work (for whatever reason) and someone is used to you taking whatever is thrown at you they will seek to restore the status quo by putting pressure on you. You continue to resist. More pressure. So you give in, 'just this once'. What you have done is taught the other person that you don't mean what you say and that they should apply more pressure more quickly next time and to keep applying pressure until you give in.

Some decisions can be made once and then stuck to, negating the need for further thought/decision-making. For example, 'I will not drink and drive' negates questions like how many drinks are legal? what can I get away with? how many have I had? how fast am I metabolizing it? what are my chances? well, I shouldn't but why not? could I find a taxi? If will-power does exist then it's certainly dissolvable in alcohol.

Small Steps

Go back to the section on goal setting (see page 41) and reconsider issues of small steps versus giant leaps. When the going gets tough knowing you can achieve the next step can be both reassuring and motivating.

Alternative Thoughts

Replace your negative, unrealistic thoughts with positive ones. Don't say 'I can't' but 'I can' (or at the very least, 'I can try'). Forget 'It's awful' or 'It's the end of the world', accept something going wrong as a minor hiccup. How to develop alternative thoughts is discussed in Chapter 7.

Role Models

Look around you at people who seem particularly good at managing their time and see what you can learn from them. Ask questions. Most people are only too happy to talk about themselves – particularly when you're telling them they're good at something. But don't feel pressurized into using their techniques if they don't suit you and your circumstances. Someone with a partner and three children is going to organize life very differently from a single person with no children.

As well as looking at people who are good role models look at those who are poor time managers. Why do you think they are? Are there similarities between your behaviour and theirs? Does their behaviour tell you things about yours you've been trying to avoid seeing?

Consequences of Behaviour

If an action brings positive consequences you are more likely to repeat it. If it brings negative consequences, including punishment, you are less likely to do it again. This sounds like common sense and is one of the few laws in psychology. Much of this chapter has been about the consequences of behaviour. When you are having difficulty changing, always look at consequences of behaviour, both of the new behaviour and the old. Even behaviour you see as a problem may have positive consequences and it is these that are maintaining it. They are not always obvious. They may have to do with controlling others, limiting the demands made on you or preserving a certain image of yourself.

Self-Image

Some of your time management problems may allow you to maintain a certain self-image. If, for example, you say 'I'm good in a crisis' this is a very positive way of describing yourself. To maintain it, and for other people to recognize it, however, you need crises in which to demonstrate your ability. Thus you will not be motivated to plan ahead, instigate progress checks, subvert problems and generally stay one step ahead if this means you lose out on shining in a crisis. To overcome this you need to be able to keep the 'I'm good in a crisis' label, but not need to demonstrate it all the time, replacing it with 'I'm good at preventing crises', or something similar.

To change successfully you may need to replace some of the positive descriptions that you currently have of yourself (but which maintain problem behaviour) with other positive descriptions which refine the new behaviour. If you don't do this you will seek to find the rewards you were getting before, through the old behaviour.

Think what these descriptions might be and how you could replace them:

- I can cope: You need to be overloaded to demonstrate this, so you don't say no
- I'm selfless/I do things for other people: This is the positive description of 'I need to be needed' – you don't say no to anything
- I'm dedicated: So you have to do everything/be overloaded
- I'm spontaneous/fun-loving: So you don't need to plan/organize yourself
- I'm creative: So you don't need to plan/organize yourself
- I'm on the fast track: So you have to take everything on/be good at everything
- I'm eccentric: So you don't have to conform to anything

⧗ PART 4

Working with Others

9

TIME AND THE CORPORATE CLIMATE

Bureaucracy is a giant mechanism operated by pygmies.
HONORÉ DE BALZAC

Inevitably when you examine what causes problems in time management you will come up with things genuinely to do with other people, the company you work for or the social or family situation in which you live. So far we have been concentrating almost exclusively on what you contribute to the problem and how to overcome this. Now it is time to turn our attention, fairly briefly, to more external causes of time management problems.

This chapter looks at factors in the company, particularly management style and its contribution to time management problems. You do not need to be a boss, however, to contribute to these problems. By simply going along with them you can reinforce the ideas and strengthen the climate you are finding it to difficult to live with. Not that challenging the organization is always the only or the best way of tackling the problem. The same thing applies in families or with groups of friends. Although the best solution for some of these problems is for management/the boss to change, this may not always be realistic. Having a better understanding of how the problem arises, and how you go along with it can, however, provide you with new ways of assessing the situation for other solutions.

Management Style and Time

The whole atmosphere of a company or department is often determined by the people at the top. Their management style will be picked up by managers further down the hierarchy and spread throughout the organization, creating stress in various guises, including time management problems. Phrases used by bosses which sum up their management style become bywords in the organization, shorthand for a whole corporate culture. (The same applies in families.) We will examine some of these styles to show how they affect the working practices, and subsequently time management, of the whole workforce. Dealing with them follows since many of the strategies fit multiple situations.

Type A Management Style

Much has been written about Type A behaviour and its relationship with stress and possible connection with heart disease (see, for example, my earlier book, *Coping with Stress at Work*). In Chapter 1, I described Type A behaviour predominately as 'hurry sickness'. There is more to the behaviour pattern than simply doing things fast and working under a sense of time pressure. Type A people are also likely to be very egotistical, dependent on external approval to confirm success, very ambitious, particularly in the material sense, to have little awareness of other people or the effects of their behaviour on others, and to have few, if any, interests outside work. Such people are also usually competitive and blame others when things go wrong, but we will examine these separately.

Here, I am less concerned with the effect of this behaviour on the individual displaying it than with its knock-on effects on others. The person who displays Type A behaviour and then collapses with a heart attack is not a good role model − even while they are showing signs of stress themselves they may still expect others to behave like them. It is the person who displays Type A behaviour successfully, who enjoys the time pressure, the heavy demands of the job and who is happy to devote their life to their job who is the real problem. The demands and expectations they make of themselves are directed at their staff, often with very negative consequences. Amongst other things they are likely to expect people to:

- Work (very) long hours – this signifies commitment
- Always put work first – even before family and certainly in front of hobbies or leisure pursuits
- Never clock watch – and this includes arranging meetings for the early evenings and weekends
- Take on all new tasks/projects without question, and often without training
- Show no signs of stress or inability to cope with everything that is thrown at them
- Never admit to problems, only to challenges
- Not ask for help, and not admit to not knowing or not being able to do something
- Not expect praise, but to shoulder criticism or blame unconditionally
- Show loyalty – not just to the company but to them. Refusal to comply with their demands is often taken personally.

The most important thing when working with or for a Type A individual is not to get sucked into their frame of reference without examining it for yourself. You may want to go back and re-examine some of your answers in Chapter 1. Do you really agree with all you said, or are you repeating the company line or saying what you know your boss would want to hear? If Type A behaviour is your normal style you may be content to leave it as such but if you feel it is being forced on you then you need to take action before it becomes an ingrained habit. I can't help but think that it is the 'forced' Type A people who are most at risk from associated health problems.

Blaming Style

When something goes wrong blaming managers are less concerned with damage limitation than with defining someone as the guilty party. Since they are not averse to making use of scapegoats this style leads to a 'cover your back' mentality in the workforce which can have disastrous consequences for time management, to say nothing of morale. In an attempt to protect themselves, staff develop many time-wasting behaviours:

- Individuals may almost totally give up verbal communication for even routine instructions/agreements/orders/discussion. Everything has to be put in writing so you have proof, should you need it.
- No one takes/wants to take decisions: the most common phrase is 'Let me check with . . .' Procrastination flourishes as no one wants to be the instigator/decision-maker who will then be blamed.
- Everything is written in triplicate (at least) – you keep a copy, one to the person involved, one to the boss, possibly your secretary keeps another copy and you may even send them to 'interested parties' (who almost certainly aren't). As well as being time consuming (memos/letters have to be typed/delivered/read/filed/replied to) it wastes other company resources.
- Trust disappears, so every story/piece of information/rumour/request is checked with as many people as possible and analysed for every reasonable and unreasonable hidden meaning.
- Innovation disappears, as change is seen to involve risk. If someone thinks there is a faster/better way of doing something they're unlikely to want to introduce it and risk reprisals when the traditional way of doing something is accepted.

Competitive Style

Our society tends to define competition as normal and healthy. It goes so far as to encourage, even demand, a competitive spirit, instilling this in children from an early age. Type A people are by definition competitive, but it can creep up on us all. We want our company to do well so we will keep our jobs – this means doing better than other companies. We want promotion, so we have to do better than others, often colleagues and co-workers. Bosses (or others) may believe fostering competition within a workforce/department (or even within a family) encourages people to do their best. Competition with those outside the company may be appropriate. In-house competition is less likely to be useful. It is counter-productive when:

- Beating another person becomes the priority rather than the job itself/productivity/other outcome measures. Time is spent planning, plotting or politicking for negative rather than positive reasons.
- Ideas/information/equipment that may benefit the department as a whole is not shared, to avoid giving others any advantage
- Deliberate delays in work occur to sabotage the 'competition'
- Only one person is seen as a 'winner' and there is no point in co-operative team effort and the rest of the staff become demoralized, and work less well or even give up
- Working longer and longer hours (but not necessarily effectively or efficiently) is seen as the way to 'win': family, leisure and health then suffer

When individual 'winning' becomes the only criterion of judgement then that will become the priority. Other priorities lose their importance, and routine tasks, where no one can shine, get ignored.

The Disorganized Boss

It's debatable which is more frustrating, bosses who know they are disorganized and inefficient but who do nothing about it, or one who is genuinely ignorant of this and its effect on others. Bosses who procrastinate, don't set realistic deadlines, don't have clear priorities, are unreliable, keep changing their minds and have unrealistic expectations of staff, can't expect the people who work for them to be making the best use of their time.

In some cases, disorganization gets relabelled crisis management. Genuine crises can occur but many are simply the result of poor planning or mismanagement. If bosses are not good time management role models, who are?

Paradoxical Demands

There is nothing permanent except change.
HERACLITUS

Increasingly, organizations give contradictory messages to their employees. Rosabeth Moss Kanter describes them in her book, *When Giants Learn to Dance*, but these paradoxical demands have been described clinically for many years. In the 1950s there was even a theory (now disproved) that schizophrenia could be caused by these type of messages, called 'double bind'. The principle is that two sets of conflicting messages are given: in personal communication this often means a discrepancy between verbal and non-verbal messages. The recipient of the message doesn't know how to respond, because whatever they do they are ignoring part of the message. Think about how you could reasonably respond to the message 'don't be so obedient'. In personal relationships this can lead to anything from frustration, anxiety, depression to a breakdown of the relationship. In a work situation the response is pretty much the same.

When people are unclear what the company's/department's real priorities are they either become dysfunctional or give up on the company and pursue their own goals. Here are some examples of common double bind messages in organizations:

- Plan for the future – but all achievement is measured in the short-term
- Be a leader/decisive/innovative – but people who rock the boat don't get promoted
- Take risks – but be prepared to be dumped if you fail
- Dedicate your life to our 'mission statement' – but give it up when the next trend comes along
- Work long hours – but don't have a heart attack on company time
- Have a spouse who is an asset to your career/the company – but don't spend any time at home

Companies are cheating themselves and their staff if they try to have it all ways. If long-term survival is the main priority then this has to be reflected in overall policy. If you want people to be flexible then this has to be built into policy and good practice. Staff, properly informed, can understand the need to react to current social, economic and political forces (even if they don't like it) and, if they see the reason, can and will adapt. Where incompetence, dithering and lack of real policy masquerades as flexibility they are likely to give up bothering.

Lean and Mean

This is not a description of Clint Eastwood but a way of justifying reducing the number of staff in a company. This is not the place to discuss issues to do with overstaffing and restructuring but it should be pointed out that some people who have time management problems cannot work more efficiently or faster. They are not machines and are already working optimally. What they need is less to do. In the last decade the hours worked by professional/managerial staff has, on average, increased to about forty-eight hours per week. In the 1960s we looked forward to a future with more leisure. Not only has this not happened, there is no reason to suppose it will happen. Except with the enforced leisure of unemployment.

The hours junior doctors work gets highlighted in the media both because they are a popular group to whom people are broadly sympathetic and because of the safety factor: no one likes the idea of being treated as an emergency by doctors who are asleep on their feet. Companies as well as individuals have to recognize that there comes a point when people simply cannot take on any more. And sometime before that they're not working at anything like their best.

Living with the Corporate Climate

Faced with a corporate culture or a management style which

contributes to time management problems what can an individual do? If you're the boss, or otherwise the cause of the problem, the answer is fairly obvious – change! If you're the one being affected by these attitudes your options may be limited. Don't get stuck in an all or nothing mode of thinking. You may not be able to change everything, to make the whole problem go away. That does not mean that you simply sit back and accept it all. Do as much as you can to improve life for yourself.

Change the Organization

It is close to impossible to get other people to change simply to benefit you. Your only real hope would be to persuade managers that their style was damaging your corporate profits: even better, damaging them and their career. For a better understanding of why organizations have problems changing, or how to effect this, read Kanter's *When Giants Learn to Dance* (see page 236). You could try unsubtle moves such as leaving this or another book open at the relevant pages around for your boss to 'find', or buying him or her a copy for Christmas. None of this will have any effect, however, unless the person involved has the insight to see that there is a problem, and then the motivation to change.

Consider Your Own Position

How secure is your job? How important is it to you? What other employment opportunities are open to you? Be realistic in this assessment and then consider how much you *really* have to put up with. Knowing you have other options can give you a greater sense of freedom to deal with the present. Do you really have to say 'yes' to every new task you are given? Try saying no. If just the thought of this makes you feel anxious pick a relatively small, unimportant task to practice with, where you can be reasonably sure the consequences of saying no won't be dramatic (see Chapter 10). But be wary of objecting and then giving in (see Chapter 8).

Challenge some of the beliefs your boss has, be they unrealistic expectations of what you can do or views about competition. If it helps, collect appropriate evidence.

Evidence

Increasingly I find people on time management workshops are already keeping some form of time log to be used as evidence of how much they do. It is not enough to simply say 'I work x hours a week, it's too much.' An immediate comeback will be that you're badly organized, incompetent or wasting a lot of time somewhere. Of more use is a time log or flow chart with multiple tasks and overlapping deadlines. Good, realistic estimates of how long things take and a plan of what you can do will be more acceptable. Even if your boss's catch phrase is 'bring me solutions, not problems' you can argue that this is what you're doing. It is not possible to get everything done (at least, not by you), so this is your solution. It helps if you can discuss priorities first, but if you can't then providing your perception of priorities might prompt him or her into responding with their views.

Open Channels of Communication

Maybe, rather than not caring, your boss doesn't realize the problems you and others are experiencing. It is never helpful to simply announce to someone what they're doing wrong, or how they're causing your problem, but some people genuinely don't see what the rest of us think must be blindingly obvious. Anything that encourages open, honest communication is likely to reap benefits (see Chapter 11).

Insecure managers are likely to be uncommunicative as a way of hiding their insecurities/lack of information/powerlessness to do anything about the situation. So are authoritarian managers who don't understand why anyone should need to know anything when they should just follow orders.

Challenge Competition

If your boss has an allergic reaction to the word 'co-operation' try using different ones (e.g. multi-disciplinary teams/reciprocal agreements . . .) as well as developing your arguments. Research evidence from social psychology and management studies shows that co-operation produces greater productivity and success, for individuals as well as departments.

The problem occurs when competition becomes a generalized response; it is applied in every situation, no matter how inappropriate. For further information and ammunition read *The Truth about Success and Motivation* by Robert Montgomery and Kanter's *When Giants Learn to Dance* which I have already mentioned (see page 236).

The competitive culture can be challenged by the development of group goals and group action.

Group Goals

These may be set formally within the company or developed by departments themselves. Anything which allows an honest discussion of objectives and goals, what the department has to do and where it is going, will begin to foster co-operative approaches rather than competition within the department. Having people involved in decision-making fosters commitment to group goals (Chapter 12) and helps people understand why decisions are made.

In some cases the only way of dealing with a particular time management problem is through group decision-making and company/department policy. In such cases, decisions tend to hinge on mutuality and reciprocity (see Chapter 10).

Pilot Scheme

If you have difficulty getting a new idea accepted put it forward as a pilot scheme or a piece or research. Suggest using a variety of outcome measures to assess whether it works: do people like it/does it get more accomplished/does it save the company money/does it cut down on time wasted . . .? Give it a limited time span to be evaluated — long enough to give it a fair try — or suggest that if it demonstrably causes problems which can't be overcome you'll revert to the old system. This method shows you've thought things through, you expect positive, measurable outcomes and you're not whingeing for the sake of it.

Different Solutions for Different Problems

Some organizations get bogged down in the change process because they want one solution/policy to cover all situations. They argue that this is 'fair'. But we accept that not everything is the same. At the very least people get different salaries, but they also work different hours, get different holidays and 'perks'. It is accepted that some jobs require shift work and night duty while others do not. There is no real reason why some time management techniques cannot be used or at least introduced on a variable basis. Bear in mind, however, that the range of jobs that can make use of the techniques is extensive; it is not just for managers.

Any organization is made up of individuals and we need to recognize that even if they share the same corporate goals, their way of achieving them might vary tremendously and they will adapt to change at different rates. An orchestra plays together to achieve a harmonious whole and we are used to the idea of different instruments playing different parts or tunes. Recently, I was at a concert and, seated so that I looked down on the orchestra, became fascinated by the habits of the violinists. All are dedicated to playing together, but some people picked up their instruments much earlier than others, tucking them under their chins and waiting, bow poised for the conductor's signal; others seemed to have a last minute dash to position their violins. Some sat expectantly on the edge of their chairs, others were more relaxed and sat well back. These variations in preparation for playing did not affect their readiness, all came together on cue. When looking at company policy on time we can't ignore that some people are always early and others are last minute, that some are tense and others relaxed, and all the other variations. By getting too hung up on the process it is easy to forget the outcome.

Work Together

Set a good example! If you start co-operating, half-way reasonable people will co-operate back. Only the most out-and-out selfishly competitive person will take advantage. If two people in a department begin to work together, co-operating where appropriate, being helpful, friendly, offering advice and constructive criticism, and are seen to be achieving, this can prompt others to follow the same path.

Type B Triumphant

A myth has developed which says that it is Type A people who get most done. This isn't true. It's just that they make more noise/are more visible and we make easy, glib connections; working long hours must mean you get more done. Sometimes it does, but not always. Type B people can do just as much, but in a more co-operative, relaxed, less high-profile way. When appropriate, or necessary, show that you are doing all that is required (or more), or as much as someone else. You just don't make such a song and dance about it.

Reassess Your Priorities

Accepting that maybe you can't 'have it all' is difficult and some people refuse to believe it. Whether you do or not is up to you. If you do continue to believe it, accept that with it comes a lot of dissatisfaction and frustration and, quite possibly, no more than an honest and realistic appraisal of your priorities. You can perform well in many roles, but you can't do *everything* in *every* role. There is a difference between having all of each role and having some of each role. Some people who work long hours, are competitive and so on, do succeed spectacularly well. They accomplish more and rise to the top and are the ones we see as role models, forgetting all those who disintegrate along the way. We can't legislate against people working long hours, having no other interests but work and reaping the benefits of this. What you do have to do is compare their lifestyle with yours. If you want the promotion and the success, what are you prepared to give up to get it? If you want time with your partner/holidays with your children/time in the garden/to sing in the local choir . . . you can't give this time to work. And you can't say 'it's not fair' when someone else makes different choices.

The Ultimate Solution

In some situations the only way to accommodate your real priorities is to leave. This is not a mark of failure, but a sign of maturity and commitment to yourself and your own priorities. This is not selfish as it might sound, because very often it means commitment to your family. The manager who has been moved around the country five times in five years may say 'no more'. Gradually companies are recognizing that this is not a sign of lack of commitment or ability but a genuine, reasoned response. And if they accept it they're likely to get a good manager who works even better.

When you can no longer accommodate the job or it can no longer accommodate you the only choice left is to go. The most notable example in recent years is British Cabinet Minister Norman Fowler's departure from Mrs Thatcher's Cabinet after ten years to, in the phrase that will always be associated will him, 'spend more time with my family'. We need more examples like this – of people who are prepared to say 'enough is enough' to balance the Mrs Thatchers of this world who say that 'home is the place to go when there is nothing better to do'.

Company Policy on Time

It is often better to change behaviour than attitudes, since a change of attitude doesn't necessarily bring with it a commensurate change in behaviour (think of the people you know who want to stop smoking but don't). Behaviour is the key to change in organizations as it is in individuals. Many problems require changes through group policy.

Flexitime

Flexitime was developed in West Germany in the 1960s and although it is most often taken to mean flexible starting and finishing time, it can be used more creatively. One section head realized that she didn't need more staff if each person worked the same number of hours in a week, but worked four long days and had a three-day weekend which enabled them to provide the cover needed. It was an idea which appealed to her staff and was instituted on a trial basis. Although jobs which involve shift changes and hand-over periods are unsuitable, most other jobs will suit various forms of flexitime, including time off for 'essentials', such as staying at home for the gas or electricity people. Core times of the day will have to be covered but this can still be flexible within parameters as decided by the group. Making good use of flexitime means that you can, for example, do your shopping at quieter times of the day. On the whole, most people find a routine and stick to it, so flexitime does not mean totally erratic work habits. What it does mean is flexibility to deal with the personal, and the unexpected.

Company Prime Time

Blocked prime time, used properly, can be so productive that some companies have instituted it as policy. A common plan is for a certain period of the day to be designated as interruption-free and all phone calls are handled by a small group of people. If this seems too much to aim for then at the very least try to get the principle of prime time established. Once a number of people block time, and see the value of it, it is easier to protect it. They don't want you to interrupt them, so they don't interrupt you. In busy offices care has to be taken that not everyone takes different times — or you can never get together — and that you're not all unavailable at the same time, unless provision for this has been made.

A company signal that everyone understands denotes prime time and that someone is not to be interrupted is useful. A common device is flags or markers which sit on desks or are placed on doors. Red means prime time and only disturb in times of dire emergency and green indicates 'I can be interrupted'. Remember almost everyone can make use of prime time on at least a semi-regular basis. Secretaries and assistants need time to do their major tasks, be it typing a complicated report full of tables to re-organizing the filing.

Empty Desks

Management which has bought the 'cluttered desk equals a cluttered mind' message will want to see clear desks. Anyone with obsessive tendencies will be pushing this idea hard. If your company has rules which say that nothing can be left on desks overnight then you will have to learn to live with it. If you're enforcing it, ask yourself why? If the office is open to public scrutiny then mess everywhere doesn't look too good; if one person's mess is disrupting other people, fair enough; but if it's only to satisfy your sense of order . . .? If you have rules about no personal objects on walls or desks, no plants, photographs, posters or holiday postcards question the rationale. Making a personal imprint on 'their' space is likely to make people feel happier and more secure, and to take more pride in it. All this contributes to good morale and thus efficiency and effectiveness. If the plants have taken over so there's no room to work or posters are offensive then they should go, but imposing a featureless, soulless, corporate environment doesn't usually do much for the human spirit, or for productivity.

A small number of companies now require people to share desks. As more people work from home or out-of-office, or work at different times, it makes sense to make maximum use of limited (and expensive) office space. People's belongings/work can be stored in small mobile cabinets which fit under desks and can be wheeled away when not in use. Japan, not surprisingly, has taken this system further than anyone else. Like other Japanese management innovations, it rests on a coherent policy supported by the prevailing culture. To introduce only part of the philosophy risks creating more problems than it solves.

10

WORKING WITH OTHERS

'If everybody would mind their own business,' said the duchess in a
hoarse growl, 'the world would go round a deal faster than it does.'
                                                      LEWIS CARROLL

When developing new time management strategies you cannot work in a vacuum, other people have to be taken into account both at work and in the family. You may have already listed some of your problems as stemming from other people, now is the time to assess how honest and realistic you were as you have more insight into what you contribute to the problem. It is also time to consider how the changes you are making affect other people and how much you respect their time. Do you, for instance, manage your time by overloading your secretary, assistant or spouse? In the long run this is not a very sensible strategy as she or he will either work less and less efficiently, become demoralized and demotivated or even leave.

Working as Part of a Team

Team building is an essential management role and skill involving leadership, communication and motivation. There is not space here to detail any of this, but suffice it to say teams that which work well together are a major advantage in not wasting individual or company time. If low morale or rapid turnover of staff contribute to your individual or departmental time management problems and you are in a managerial position then developing these skills is a necessary step. If it is your boss who is the problem then the solution is more difficult and more varied, depending on the company. Anything which encourages companies to invest in staff training, including managerial skills, is to be welcomed.

Schedule regular time with the team or your secretary/assistant to sort out priorities/give or get information/get questions answered/go over details ... Such a meeting should happen on a daily basis with your secretary and shouldn't take longer than five to fifteen minutes. Not knowing what is going on or not being kept informed is a secretary's most common complaint and an important source of time-wasting.

Delegating

Delegating is a major role of management — it is getting things done, achieving objectives, through other people. Delegating does not mean passing on things you don't want to do, be they difficult, boring or risky. Delegating is giving people the authority to carry out tasks or projects. Delegating means passing on pleasant tasks as well as unpleasant — high profile, rewarding tasks as well as low profile, maintenance tasks. Delegating is part of team building and also part of a person's development as they take on new tasks and learn new skills and responsibilities. Delegating is a powerful tool in time management, not only because it frees your time for other things, but also because it forces you to plan and organize. If you're to delegate tasks or projects to others you have to give them a clear outline, including their area of authority/responsibility, set deadlines and initiate a feedback system whereby you can monitor progress. You also have to assign tasks and responsibilities to those most able to handle them, which involves knowing your staff sufficiently well. This includes their personal aspirations, since if a person feels they're involved in something which will develop their career they are likely to be better motivated.

Delegating might mean that you and the people you're delegating to will need to develop a training package/schedule to allow them to learn the necessary skills. Since it does not absolve you of responsibility you need to do it well, which includes having trust in the person to whom you give the work.

If you're still worried about delegating, or resisting the whole idea, list the reasons why. Many of the fundamental, underlying reasons we've already mentioned and by now you should be able to spot what they are. You should also be noticing that the same reasons come up over and over again for you, in different guises. Insecurity, perfectionism, need for control, need to be of service or need to be busy will be a thread running through each of the sections.

We only need to briefly recap the underlying reasons for lack of delegating since we are now, in the main, reinforcing ideas you've come across before.

Insecurity

You're worried that by giving staff greater responsibility they will outstrip you/do the task better than you/prove you're unnecessary. You may also believe that the only way to prove your worth is not to allow other people a chance. This means that you will avoid giving people the opportunity to show what they can do and/or you will avoid training people. Getting on is as much about creating a good team and bringing people up with you as it is shining as an individual.

You might have some transient insecurities if you are in a new job and unclear of your current responsibilities and unsure of your colleagues. These will usually be overcome by trial and error, giving people a chance, within limits, and monitoring outcome. If you persist in using this as an excuse you're covering up for other reasons.

Control

When you do get round to delegating you over-supervise and don't allow people any creativity or choices about what they do. It is less a matter of delegating than it is of giving people a detailed set of instructions from which they must not deviate. Your need to know exactly what is happening may stem from insecurity. Or, if you equate control with power and power with success, then giving up control/power will be experienced as diminishing. You are likely to see other people 'gaining' — in experience, skill or enjoyment through responding to a challenge — as you are 'losing'.

Perfectionism

The 'I can do it better myself' syndrome we have already discussed (see page 122).

Lack of an Overview

It is difficult to delegate effectively if you lack perspective on what needs to be done. Your lack of an overview might include not just your own goals and priorities, but your department's or the company's. Bad or no planning or organization can mean that you end up doing things yourself because everything is such a mess and deadlines are so short no one else is even prepared to try.

Altruism

'Why should I ask someone else to do it?' This type of response usually means you're only seeing delegation in terms of 'nasty' tasks, or passing on things you don't want to do. It can also be used as a way to disguise keeping people down (see Control, page 131) because you say 'I can't promote them/pay them overtime' without giving them the chance to decide for themselves whether they still might benefit from the task.

'They Can't Do It'

If this is a genuine assessment of the situation you're probably already taking steps to rectify the position through training. If you're not, one of the other reasons is the genuine one.

'What Will I Do?'

You're worried that if you successfully delegate work, and furthermore, if your staff are competent at it, your bosses will begin to wonder if they really need you. This probably means you're not clear what your role/job description is. You need to sort this out and spend time developing your job and your potential rather than just holding on to everything, no matter how trivial.

Need to be Needed

This is often allied to the above category – you get satisfaction from other people needing you. If you see yourself very much as someone who cares for and nurtures others, and you do this primarily by doing things, you will be very loath to give them up.

'I'm Achieving'

You equate activity with accomplishment, to the extent that you can lose sight of your goals as you rush around being busy. Thus you see any delegation of activities as loss of possible 'achievement'. You can't bear to give anything up because you equate running around frantically as a sign of success/importance.

Why Delegate?

Having looked at why you don't delegate let us consider for a moment reasons why you should:

- It gives you more time to do higher priority tasks/develop your job/do the things you want to do
- It can motivate staff and help them develop a team spirit/a sense of belonging/a sense of being trusted or valued if they are given interesting, stimulating work

- It can improve people's skills, confidence and competence, which then . . .
- . . . increases your department's/company's productivity
- Someone else might do the task *better* (or faster) than you
- If you drop dead through stress of overwork someone knows what has to be done/can carry on

How to Delegate

1. Give clear information/instructions. This doesn't mean telling your staff exactly how to do something, but it does mean outlining parameters of authority and responsibility, giving deadlines, setting standards and discussing supervision, feedback and evaluation.
2. Make sure you both have the same understanding of what you've agreed (see Chapter 11).
3. Explain why something has to be done – the more you're asking of someone, the shorter the deadlines, the more important this will be. Also explain how it fits into the bigger picture.
4. Make sure the person has adequate skills or arrange for any special training they need.
5. Allow as much autonomy or creativity as you can. This both makes doing the job easier and increases satisfaction.
6. Check that the person being delegated to doesn't just see this as an additional, stressful burden and that they have time to do it. This may mean they have to delegate tasks/duties of their own.
7. Devise a system both you and the person doing the task can live with which gives you a regular update on what is happening. This means you don't lose track and worry, nor do you suddenly discover nothing has been done.
8. Give support, encouragement and praise as and when needed, including regular supervision of what is going on, but don't be constantly looking over their shoulder. Praise in public; if you have to criticize do so privately.
9. At the end go over the task with the person, giving specific

comments/praise so that the person can learn from it.
10. Within a team/department, delegate work equitably.

When Not to Delegate

- When it's a rotten job that you don't want to do
- When it involves confidential information that should not go beyond you
- When you let the person come back to you with all the problems so you end up doing most of the task anyway
- When it involves anything to do with discipline/criticism
- When you shouldn't be doing it anyway – you don't want to delegate it, you need to get it permanently reassigned elsewhere.

Interruptions

Sometimes it seems as though everyone wants some of your time, and they want it *now*. Interruptions from other people come mainly via the telephone and by people arriving to see you without an appointment, whether it is your boss/colleague/neighbour/the gas man ... They break in on what you're doing. How you handle interruptions depends on a number of factors – whether you have a secretary or someone who can divert them, whether part of your job is to deal with interruptions and, lastly, what else is going on at the time.

To start analysing the kinds of interruptions you get and your response to them, look at your time log and mark all the interruptions. Now rate them for urgency and importance. This involves assessing, among other things, consequences, time scales, who was doing the interrupting and how it complements your goals/priorities. Now look at the amount of time you spent on the interruption, including how long it took to pick up the task you stopped, and ask yourself 'Was it worth it?'

Sometimes the answer is yes, but more often it is no. What makes the difference? Were there times you allowed an interruption to happen, or even encouraged it, because you were bored/fed-up/doing something difficult/doing something you didn't like? Often we are more than happy for someone to interrupt us because it is light relief in an otherwise hum-drum day. But if on Monday we welcome someone who interrupts, chats for fifteen minutes and we let them go only with reluctance we should not be surprised if they come back on Tuesday. Nor should we be surprised if, when we indicate we don't have time to chat, they act confused/surprised/hurt/annoyed/put-out.

It is unlikely that one, entirely consistent policy towards interruptions will be appropriate, so it is important that you can quickly assess the situation and then give an unambiguous message regarding your position.

Some interruptions are part, if not the whole, of your job and often they will occur in the form of emergencies. As a nurse or doctor in an accident and emergency department your day is a series of unexpected problems – unexpected in the sense that you don't know exactly what is coming, all you know is that something will arrive. If you're a fireman 'interruptions' are the basis of your job, and these punctuate the time waiting for them to happen. If you are any kind of troubleshooter then emergencies are your working life and should not properly be seen as interruptions. This does not stop some people experiencing them as such.

This might also be true on a less dramatic scale. Is dealing with interruptions part of your job, whether these are queries/complaints/requests . . .? If you are in any type of service job the answer may well be yes, but you need to ask, is it for every minute of every day? You've always had an open door policy for your staff/students/friends . . . does this have to be all day, everyday? Realistically assess where you may be able to set limits. If you feel guilty turning others away, in fact saying 'no' to them, this may indicate problems with assertiveness. This is the issue which will have to be tackled if you are to have much success in instituting a new system.

In many cases you can set limits to the amount of time you will be available. If you're blocking time this is the time you will want to try to protect from interruptions. How might you do this?

Share Interruptions

Offer to take all interruptions – phone calls, individuals requiring help or information or whatever – for a colleague for a given length of time if they will do the same for you. For example, in a busy library one or more people can be freed from readers enquiries for a given period allowing them to complete other tasks. This only works if the person can deal with the majority of the queries, can handle the volume of traffic (or can quickly get help if needed) and doesn't expect to accomplish anything else during this time. We see examples of this all the time in shops and smaller supermarkets when the sole cashier calls for help when the queue gets to a certain size.

Appointments

Make use of an appointment system whenever possible. For this to work people need to be able to see you reasonably quickly, you have to keep appointments and there has to be some leeway for genuine emergencies. If you try to put people off for several weeks, cancel appointments or are habitually late then you can't expect other people to honour them either.

When setting appointments try to get some idea why someone wants to see you (respecting the fact that they may not always want to divulge this to a secretary if this is the person they make the appointment with) and set an appropriate deadline. Appointments may seem formal, or a way of distancing yourself, but if you have people queuing to see you, or trying to catch you on a hit-or-miss basis, think how much of their time you save by eliminating waiting, as well as protecting your own time. And saving their time maximizes the productivity of your department. Think of the difference between a well-run appointments system at your doctor's surgery and the old days when you were seen in the order you arrived and could wait hours.

Meetings

If you are interrupted by a number of people with similar problems or problems relating to the same project either set up a meeting to clarify the issues involved or use a regular departmental meeting to do this. If you don't have regular, short staff meetings to deal with departmental/company business, consider whether this might be productive. Although most of us have a (sensible) tendency to avoid even more meetings, they can deal with many interruption problems which stem from general ignorance – about projects, who might be more appropriate to sort out a query, unclear instructions or expectations of others, and so on. To ensure a non-time wasting meeting see Chapter 12.

Honesty

If you really don't have time to deal with a casual visitor say so rather than ungraciously give them half your attention and constantly look at your watch. They will usually prefer all your attention at a later date rather than part of your attention immediately. Suggest another time to them and don't then put it off.

If you tell someone you are busy and they persuade you to talk to them saying 'It'll only take a couple of minutes', and you allow the interruption to drag on for half an hour, you are teaching them that you don't mean what you say and you are open to interruptions at any time. Either make them stick to their 'couple of minutes' or ask them to come back later.

Hide

If all else fails, and you have something that simply has to be done go somewhere else. Possibilities are conference rooms, company libraries, borrowing someone else's office (with their phone switched through to their secretary) in another part of the building or even sitting in your car in the car park. If you have the freedom to leave the building you can work at home or in a public reference library. You can even go to the extreme of going away. One writer I know hires a remote caravan on a Scottish island well away from distractions, including telephones, shops, people, electricity and running water, and camps out to get work done.

Another alternative is to come to work early or stay late and thus avoid phones and people. Be wary of doing this on a regular basis as it can quickly come to be seen as your normal practice and then you find your 'quiet time' taken up by people who know you'll be there and this is a good time to catch you.

Go to Them

If possible go to other people rather than have them come to you. It's easier to control the time spent when you are the one who has to walk away.

Stand Up

Rather than let someone flop down in a seat and get comfortable stand up when they come in. Few people will then sit and they are less likely to linger if you keep them standing.

Don't Invite Interruptions

The more often you interrupt others, or welcome their interruptions with cups of coffee as a way of putting things off, the stronger the message you are giving about interruptions being acceptable.

Leaving your door open, facing it, looking up and smiling at everyone who walks past invites interruptions. So does opening the door to a neighbour at home and immediately saying 'come in' and leading the way to the kitchen for coffee. You don't have to be unfriendly to indicate you don't have time to be interrupted, but the more open you are the more people will assume you can be. Walking briskly, along the street or the corridor, and not slowing as you approach people you know indicates you don't have time to stop, but you can still look them in the eye, smile and say hello without breaking stride. The more you saunter, stroll or roam around the more you look as though you are in search of an interruption.

If necessary rearrange your furniture so you don't face the door, or shut the door. Don't have a convenient, comfortable chair for someone to sit in. In an open-plan office, use filing cabinets, screens or bushy plants to give you some protection from catching the eye of every passer-by.

Some people need to carry a pager but many more do so because they feel it lends them an air of importance. It seems to act as a signal for them, 'Look, I'm so important I have to be available all the time.' The implication is that they have 'to make vital decisions'. It could, however, be interpreted as 'you're at everyone's beck and call'. Increasingly, the image conveyed by people carrying mobile phones is not one of importance, but of 'self-importance' or insecurity. Really important people know that whoever is trying to contact them will ring back. Advertisements which indicate you no longer have to get out of the bath to answer the phone imply that: (a) you have to answer the phone no matter what you are doing; (b) it's all right to be interrupted in the bath; and even (c) why expect to be left alone to have a bath in peace and quiet. Carrying a cellular phone tells people you expect, even welcome, interruptions.

Assertiveness

It is easy to say that the biggest help in managing your time is to say 'no', but this assumes that you can. Several times I've mentioned that assertiveness may be a problem and, although to do justice to this important skill would take a book in its own right, a number of brief points can be made. The first is to make it absolutely clear that assertiveness isn't the same as aggression and to show how it differs from non-assertion.

Aggressive Behaviour

Aggression is getting your own way, no matter what the cost. Aggression is riding roughshod over others: it is the 'weakest to the wall' mentality. Aggression may get you what you want in the short term, but it usually brings long-term problems as others cease to want to work with you/trust you/co-operate with you. You may not care if they don't like you, but lack of trust or co-operation or even unwillingness to deal with you can spell isolation and downfall. You're being aggressive (not assertive) if you:

- Deal with issues in a confrontational, 'I win, you lose' manner
- Magnify disagreements and play down agreement
- State your opinion as fact
- Insist on your 'rightness' and won't discuss options
- Dismiss other people's ideas/opinions/values as worthless
- Deal with differences of opinion with sarcasm and hostility

Non-assertive Behaviour

You may feel being non-assertive adds to your time management problems by overloading you but has positive pay-offs because, for example, since you don't say no to people, they like you. Is this really true? Does it work like that? If you do something half-heartedly because you weren't committed in the first place, or do something badly so you won't get asked to do it again, you are more likely to get a poor reputation, for being unreliable/slow/incompetent/indecisive. Most people would rather have a clear answer, even a negative, than weeks of 'maybe'. You're being non-assertive when you:

- Dismiss your ideas/views/values/emotions as worthless or less important than other people's
- When you don't openly disagree but don't do what the other person now expects you to do
- When you express anger or hostility indirectly through acts of sabotage, rather than openly

- When you only express your views apologetically
- When you don't make decisions because you might hurt/offend someone

Assertive Behaviour

Assertiveness means understanding your rights and standing up for them without infringing on the rights of others. It means valuing your own ideas/opinions/viewpoint/emotions and expressing them appropriately. It also means taking responsibility for yourself and your emotions, not blaming others – 'You make me so angry . . .' The assertive person does not undervalue themself or put themself down, but neither do they undervalue others or put them down. You are being assertive when you:

- Accept that both you and others have the right to your own opinions/ideas/values, and that these may be different . . .
- . . . and that sometimes they are not right or wrong, simply different
- Can express your honest opinion without it leading to conflict
- Can disagree with others and have them disagree with you without it leading to conflict
- Believe in your own self-worth

Although assertiveness is as much about beliefs and attitudes as it is about behaviour, it also has to be seen in relation to culture and gender. The British will probably always apologize and explain more than the Australians and the Americans. Although it can be deeply frustrating to women to have their assertive behaviour, which may not be remarkable in a man, described as aggressive, this has to be borne in mind when examining outcomes. It is demoralizing to have positive advances characterized in this negative way.

Refusing requests

Refusing inappropriate requests is likely to be part of any time management strategy. The beliefs that underpin a non-assertive response, saying 'yes' when you really want to say 'no' are likely to be:

- Nice people do things for others – it would be rude/selfish to say no
- They are more important than me so I have to say yes
- I haven't the right to say no
- If I say no they'll be hurt/angry/offended
- If I say no they won't like me

If you add to these other beliefs which cause people to say 'yes', such as wanting to feel important/to be busy/to be involved/needing to feel needed, it is easy to see how people become overloaded. While your basic beliefs need challenging (see Chapter 7) there are some techniques for assertively refusing requests:

- Don't say 'maybe' when you mean 'no'. A straightforward no at the outset is usually easiest . . .
- . . . however, in some circumstances you may want to ask for more time so you can think things through/look at deadlines/consider priorities and options. In such cases, it is a genuine request to aid a decision, not a delaying tactic or non-assertion.
- Ask for more information/clarification if this helps decision-making: 'What is the deadline?', 'Who else is involved?'
- Keep replies short, but not abrupt – the more you ramble the more you'll tie yourself in knots. A simple 'no', however, can, in many circumstances, sound abrupt, rude or offhand . . .
- . . . give the real reason for refusing, not an excuse – whether it is 'I can't because . . ', 'I don't want to' or simply 'It's not my scene'. Saying 'I can't . . .' can sound like an excuse, but is justified if you're saying 'I would have done, but can't this time because my time is presently committed.' If you mean 'I'll never want to do this . . .' then 'I can't . . .' is an excuse.
- You may feel more comfortable saying 'I'm sorry . . .' but don't over-apologize

- If someone has given you the opportunity to do something (rather than off-loading something on you) thank them, even if you have to say no
- Keep communication channels open, through explanation/thanks, if you want to be involved in the future or would welcome similar opportunities
- Make sure your nonverbal behaviour matches your verbal – no saying 'maybe' (or even 'no') while your nonverbal behaviour communicates something else
- Use 'I' statements rather than hide behind rules or other people: 'My mum won't let me' may be acceptable when we're children but as adults we have to make, and stand by, our own decisions

The Impact of Your Behaviour on Others

Do as you would be done by is the surest method of pleasing.
PHILIP DORMER STANHOPE, EARL OF CHESTERFIELD

When you make changes to your behaviour it has an inevitable knock on effect for other people. Although this may be positive – you get to spend more time with your family, which you all want – in some cases the change will affect someone adversely. If it causes them problems they will try to maintain the status quo and stop you changing. If you're to succeed in your new behaviour you need to consider how it affects others beyond 'Does it give them more work?' How does your change affect others? It can:

- Inconvenience them: The obvious way is when it gives them more work, but in some subtle ways it can mean that you are less accessible to them (appointments rather than open door), less sociable (no more chatting whenever they want) or you are removing your support (you're not always available/you limit your time).
- Challenge them: You're doing something about your time management problems and it makes them uncomfortable because they're in the same mess but doing nothing.

- Threaten them: If you get better control of your time you will be more successful/achieve more/'overtake' them.

In all these instances the other person will apply pressure to get you to drop your new behaviour. How might they do this?

- With threats: These are quite straightforward, and usually of the type 'If you do/don't . . . then I'll . .' Depending on how much power the other person has to exercise sanctions this might or might not be successful. Sometimes people try to use it positively: I've had people on my time management courses because their wives have insisted (because they see so little of then because of long hours of work) and even because secretaries have insisted – which seems a very powerful motivator.
- With emotional blackmail: In families this is usually expressed as 'If you really loved me you'd . .' In other situations it can be more subtle, as when someone says 'As a favour to me . .' and implies that if you refuse you're rejecting them.
- By teasing: Your capacity to change is undermined: 'I don't know why you bother . . . it won't work', 'You can't do it' or 'How many times have you tried this before?'
- By refusing to take you seriously: Closely allied to teasing, the message is 'You're OK as you are' and 'So you're a slob/always late/never finishing things . . . we love you anyway.'
- With('helpful') criticism: This is often the most annoying means of putting on pressure – 'You really shouldn't take on so much' when you're trying to shed tasks/learn how to say no/sort out your priorities.
- Through indifference: After the above, this may seem a blessing, but most of us want some help or reward, or, at the very least, awareness, from our nearest and dearest if no one else.

Dealing with these behaviours means tackling them head on, and this starts with honest and open communication. Explain to colleagues that you're not rejecting them, and why the change is important to you. Don't cut yourself off, you can stay social but in more a controlled way. Explain how serious you are about the change where appropriate and if people continue to undermine your efforts question their motives. Very often it is a response to feeling threatened. Ask yourself whether dealing with this is your problem or theirs. If it's your partner you may want to discuss it. If it's colleagues you may decide it is up to them to deal with it themselves. Above all, once you've decided on a course of action, don't let others talk you out of it. You'll only teach them you don't mean what you say, and next time it will be even harder.

11

COMMUNICATION

When you have nothing to say, say nothing.
CHARLES CALEB COLTON

More time is wasted because of poor communication than anything else but poor planning. How many times have you had to do something again because you misunderstood the first time, or had to ask someone to redo a task because somewhere along the line wires had got crossed? What about the time wasted when you go off in a huff at some imagined slight the other person wasn't even aware of? Or when negotiations break down because of misunderstanding? What about the time wasted because you thought you knew what someone was thinking – and discovered too late that you didn't? And then there's all the paper you have to keep track of, letters, memos, reports, faxes, the company newsletter, to say nothing of journals, magazines, articles and books that keep us up to date, or help us to move into new areas.

There are many ideas and theories about interpersonal communication. Some hold that almost all emotional and interpersonal problems stem from problems in communication and thus take a psychotherapeutic solution. Now is not the time to discuss such approaches. Communication is a two-way process involving three parts, the source of the message (you/the company newsletter/ a memo from your boss/your child . . .), the message itself and the person receiving the message (you/your partner/your boss . . .). These three factors interact in various ways to produce endless nuances in communication style. They need expert awareness in many areas of specialist communication, be it public speaking/ advertising a new product/negotiating pay settlements/selling a service/talking to a patient/giving out safety instructions on an aircraft.

From a time management point of view we can concentrate on three issues. The first has to do with comprehension. Are you being understood? Are you accurately understanding others? The second is channels of communication. How do you get your message across? Lastly, we can look at overload. How much communication/ information do you need and how much can you deal with?

Comprehension

'Then you should say what you mean,' the March Hare went on.
'I do,' Alice hastily replied: 'at least — at least I mean what I say — that's the same thing, you know.'
'Not the same thing a bit!' said the Hatter. 'Why, you might just as well say that 'I see what I eat' is the same as 'I eat what I see!'

LEWIS CARROLL

All of us, no doubt, have at some time had a conversation with someone which felt as though it belonged with Alice on one of her strange adventures. Somehow, what we were saying wasn't interpreted by the other person in the way we meant it. Usually we put it down to the other person's obtuseness. Or we can't understand what someone is telling us — either new ideas or instructions — and we assume they don't have clear ideas, or they lack communication skills.

Why does communication break down? Why are some messages incomprehensible?

Nonverbal Communication

There is not space here to examine the whole area of nonverbal communication. Nonverbal behaviour, or body language, is the way we communicate without language. It includes facial expression, gesture, use of space, touching, posture, appearance and tone of voice.

Although there has been a lot of research on this topic, anyone who pretends to be able to tell you what every little twitch and gesture means is exaggerating our knowledge. That is not to say that this area isn't worth some investigation and is vital if you have real communication problems (see page 236 for suggested reading).

The important thing to understand for now is congruence. Does your nonverbal behaviour give the same message as your words? If someone isn't taking you seriously, or is ignoring what you are saying, maybe it is because you are giving mixed messages with your body.

If, for example, you are saying 'No, I don't want to do that' and this message is being ignored, is it because your nonverbal behaviour is saying 'I don't mean what I say'? I have seen people say 'no' while nodding their heads: a secretary perhaps who says, 'No, I want to get away on time tonight' at the same time taking the cover off her typewriter in preparation to doing some more work; or people saying how angry and upset they are while they continue to smile. Where conflicting messages are given it is generally accepted that the nonverbal message is the 'true' one. Why else would men accused of rape use (and sometimes get away with) the excuse 'I didn't think she meant what she said'? Whilst this is an extreme example it does bring home the gravity of unclear messages.

Sometimes the 'true' message is nonverbal, but often it is a mixture of both the verbal and nonverbal. Someone is saying they don't want to do the extra work, they are angry or upset. One part of them means this, but they are preparing to do the extra work and this gets taken as the 'truth'. The nonverbal message is not always the opposite of what is said, but an indication that the person is uncomfortable about expressing negative messages. Cultural conditioning means women are more likely than men to have difficulty in conveying negative messages and will look uncomfortable. Sometimes this is expressed in reverse, as when a person agrees to do something, but they sigh, their shoulders droop, they pull a face, their tone of voice is flat, everything about them says they're unenthusiastic. Check it out. If people don't understand you, is it your words or your non-verbal behaviour which is creating the problem? Are you articulating the company message you don't really believe? This will come through.

As the comedian Frank Carson so frequently reminds us of his jokes: 'It's the way I tell 'em!'

Listening

Listening is a much underestimated skill. Anyone can do it – all you have to do is sit there. Not so. You're not listening if while the other person is talking you have turned off and are gazing into space/daydreaming/planning your next clever remark. Egocentric people are poor listeners. Listening is an active process which requires you to: (i) take in what the other person says; (ii) think about it: and (iii) *check what is meant.*

This can involve clarifying the statement/question as well as asking for supplementary information: 'Give me your comments on this report' can mean anything from 'Write a reply', 'Give me a few headings', 'I don't understand this, do you?' to 'Is this really right?' You can either guess or try for some clarification. Although occasionally people are being deliberately vague to cover their lack of knowledge/information/understanding, in most cases clarifying what is meant is welcomed as useful.

The three basic steps are:

1. Ask open-ended questions/for more details – this shows you are paying attention: 'In what way do you think I'm disorganized?'
2. Check your understanding: 'Are you saying I'm disorganized?'
3. Don't let your mind drift off: 'If you think this is disorganized you should have seen the person I shared an office with a few years ago ... what was his name ... lovely wife ... much brighter than him ... wonder where they are now ..?'

Listening also means acknowledging what you have heard. Don't ask for feedback if you intend to do nothing with it. If you do get feedback but you can't act on it, explain why. Acknowledging that you have heard, and understood, someone's point of view is important to them. Avoid the expression 'I hear you' unless you're involved in person-oriented psychotherapy since it is invariably accompanied by the nonverbal message 'but I'm not paying any attention'/'I really don't care'.

Can *not* listening ever be useful? Some people bulldoze their way through a difficult encounter by talking more than they listen. Although this may have the short-term advantage of not having to answer awkward questions, the nonverbal message is 'I have something to hide.'

Mind Reading

Listening doesn't mean mind reading. Checking out means more than clarifying a message, it can involve examining a whole set of assumptions. Don't assume that you know, for a fact, what motivates another person, why they behave as they do. Sometimes you may be right, often you're wrong. Often we are egocentric in our mind reading and assume that a person's behaviour relates to us. Someone may be offhand with you because you've offended them but maybe they're offhand because they're preoccupied – they're worried about their children/had a row with their partner/annoyed with their boss/had a near miss with another car on their way to work/are hungover/have 'flu coming on/are involved with an interesting problem/are desperate to get to the toilet . . .

If you're concerned, ask: 'You seem a bit offhand. Have I done something to offend you?' If you have, most people are glad of the opportunity to say so and clear the air. If they're not, they don't then owe you an explanation of what is bothering them. If you're egocentric be prepared to be disappointed by how little you feature as a cause of other people's behaviour.

Clarity

If any man wishes to write in a clear style, let him first be clear in his thoughts.

JOHANN W. VON GOETHE

Much time is wasted, and confusion caused, by people ignoring Goethe's advice and that of Colton at the beginning of the chapter. Assuming you do have something to say, and you are clear what it is, say it as simply as possible. Avoid jargon, long words and convoluted grammar unless you are absolutely sure it is appropriate and will be understood. If you're doing it to impress others make sure you've got the criteria right. Substance is usually more important than form in the sense that you can't disguise poor ideas by dressing them up. At the same time you don't want good ideas to get lost because no one understands you. Clarity of ideas is always impressive.

Organize your thoughts and present them in a logical order and only make a limited number of points at a time. This is true whether you're talking to one person, a small meeting or a large gathering. What is the most important thing you want to convey? If you're rambling, using too many words, in speech or in writing, ask yourself these questions:

- Is it necessary or is it extra detail?
- Is it factual or am I giving my opinions? Is that appropriate?
- Is it relevant or have I digressed?
- Is it clear?

Channels of Communication

Whether something is formal or informal, direct or indirect, is often outside our control and dictated by the system or the situation. Most people prefer a briefing session where they can ask questions to a notice being pinned up on a board. Company newsletters can be useful, but there is no guarantee they are read by everyone. *Cascading* is current jargon for one person telling a group of people each of whom then tell another group and so on. This can work well if everyone has sufficient understanding and receives clear information for messages not to get mixed. Most of us played Chinese Whispers as children and know how easily messages get altered. Cascading tends to be better at sending messages down a chain than it does in getting feedback coming back up.

There are some channels we all use and can't avoid.

Memos

Memos should be short, clear, to the point, and limited in what they try to do. Unless memos are only going to a few close colleagues who you know will understand your sense of humour, it is best to be straightforward. Sarcasm and irony are often misinterpreted in the memo and you don't want to add to confusion. Jokey memos can likewise give conflicting messages. In all cases, it is the nonverbal element that is missing. People usually need to know you well to put this back in and to understand it.

Memos can be a reminder, give information or suggest dates for a meeting but they can't take the place of a discussion or debate to exchange ideas. The majority of memos people get are glanced at and thrown away (or put on one side, and forgotten) as being of little relevance. Many people 'cc' too much: if we're not sure who to put on a circular list we tend to include names. Thus everyone gets too many memos which we're not sure why we've got or what we're supposed to do with them.

If you send copies to people as a way of drawing what you're doing to their attention make sure it doesn't backfire. Irrelevant information can annoy people and they feel you're wasting their time. Send copies to people working on the relevant project or who will be affected by it (directly or indirectly). Make it clear whether the memo is to be acted upon (give a deadline, say 'for action' or 'for decision') or whether it is for information only. If you send memos to people above your boss send your boss a copy also, to indicate this is open communication and you're not being devious. Follow company style in listing names (if it uses a hierarchical approach) or simply list names alphabetically.

If you want to cut down on the time you waste with memos don't expect to get every memo your colleague gets, and don't complain that you're being left out when you don't get something irrelevant. Ask yourself how necessary it is for you to have that piece of information. If the answer is 'very' do something about it. If you're simply being nosy let it go.

Telephone

How much time do you spend a day on the telephone? Estimate and then check with your time log. Does it seem excessive? How much of this is productive use of time? How much is chatting?

Most of us are conditioned to answer the phone the moment it rings, no matter what we are doing. Every time you leap to answer the phone you are reacting to someone else's priorities. In a work situation you might be unable to let a phone ring and not answer it, but at home do you always have to answer it? If it's important the caller will ring back. You might even want to consider an answering machine at home as well as work to relieve you of some of the pressure.

The section on interruptions (see pages 175–180) suggests some ideas for a rotation system by which different people answer the phone for certain hours, giving everyone a period of peace and quiet. If this isn't appropriate for you and you don't have an answering machine or a secretary to screen calls, you'll have to learn to minimize the interruption value:

- Let the phone ring while you make a note of where you are so you can return to what you're doing more easily
- Ask how you can help someone which encourages specific requests
- Say you're busy/in a meeting/have someone with you and you'll get back to them
- If you don't want to chat don't ask questions like 'How are you?' or 'How's it going?' which encourages people to tell you – in detail
- If it's someone you know is likely to ramble tell them you only have a couple of minutes before you have to leave – then stick to it

For the best use of the phone:

- Block calls, keep a list and make a group of calls together. It is easier not to chat when you know you're going on to another call. It also means you interrupt yourself less often if one of the calls is engaged: you can retry between each call.
- If you're calling another person ask them whether this is a convenient time to talk. The gesture is appreciated and is usually reciprocated. This makes saying 'No, not now' easier and should always be followed by 'But you can get me at . . ?'
- Make a note of what you want to talk to someone about, so you can cover two, three or even four points in one call. Or you can cover these points when you are interrupted without stretching your memory.
- If your tendency is to chatter, keep an egg-timer by the phone – for most people this is unnecessary and makes them self-conscious
- Get in the habit of saying 'Can I call you back?' if you're working and don't want to have to stop
- Say 'I have to go now' – and go
- Say 'One last point . . ?' – and don't add more
- If all else fails pretend someone has come in/knock on your desk and act as though someone is at the door/buy a gadget which provides a selection of interruption sounds, including a secretary saying you're wanted elsewhere

Learn to use all the extras which your phone might have: redial facilities, call forward, memory for numbers, and so forth. If you've got them you might as well use them. Bear in mind you can replace some meetings with conference calls.

Answering Machines

But answer came there none.

SIR WALTER SCOTT

Although getting a recorded message instead of the person you want to talk to is annoying it is usually better than no reply at all. For people/places where you know there will be an answering machine, be ready with your message. Be clear, concise and, most important, tell them who you are, where and when you can be contacted. Sensible use of an answering machine can prevent time being wasted playing telephone tag.

You can use your own answering machine, not just to take calls when you're not there, but to avoid being interrupted and to filter calls. Remote control devices allow you to access your messages from anywhere with a phone. You should avoid, however, taking this gadget on holiday with you.

Praise and Blame

In seeking to change the behaviour of others rewards work better than punishment. Rewards can also be used to motivate. A common complaint from people who are dissatisfied at work is that they are not appreciated. This doesn't just mean not being paid enough, or not being promoted, but includes not being appreciated on a more basic, day-to-day level. Giving people feedback, telling them what they're doing right, as well as what they're doing wrong, acknowledges them as individuals as well as aiding the learning process, and this contributes to more harmonious working and personal relationships.

Beware, however, of flinging the odd word of praise or encouragement out inappropriately – if you are not sincere it will show in your nonverbal behaviour (unless you are a skilled actor) and is likely to do more damage than good. People will feel you are simply trying to manipulate or take advantage of them and this causes resentment.

Getting Feedback From Staff

This can be obtained from anything from surveys to departmental meetings, informal chatting to the cascade working in reverse.

Feedback from staff includes everything from general opinion surveys to detailed discussions on projects/ideas/products/management strategies. Depending on what you want opinions about, you could try a computerized survey which takes the individual through a set of questions and can guarantee anonymity, or discussion groups, possibly run by an outside (at least outside the department) consultant targeted on a particular problem and aimed at getting practical solutions.

Asking staff what they think can integrate them into a team and can contribute to their feelings of involvement, but only if this is acted upon. Asking for feedback and then ignoring it is worse than not asking. If there are reasons why it can't be acted upon, these should be explained.

The Personal Touch

Sometimes taking a little longer to do something can be worthwhile. Although many people these days don't subscribe to the belief that personal letters should be handwritten (those who still take the time to write letters, that is), there are some occasions when it is worth it, as well as good manners. Thank-you letters should be handwritten. And remember to say, or write, thank-you notes – particularly when people have put themselves out for you. Most of us remember to say or write thank you for things, but for busy people the most precious thing they can give you is their time. One man called on to speak to charities frequently reported that he was more likely to put himself out for groups who wrote a thank-you note than for those who simply accepted it as their due.

Writing to people personally shows you've appreciated their efforts, and handwritten notes indicate that you appreciate it enough to take the time to acknowledge it yourself, rather than delegate this to a secretary. One woman involved in organizing a charity art exhibition filled in people's names on the invitation by hand. A surprising number of people commented on 'how civilized' this was.

Talking to people rather than sending a memo may or may not save time. Weigh up the cost-benefits in terms of interruptions, the creation of more paperwork, with its attendant problems, versus the personal touch.

Information Overload

In our fast moving, ever changing world new information is coming at us constantly. And we make the mistake of trying to keep up with it. The gap between what you can understand/know and what you think you should understand/know has been called information anxiety. Information is hurled at us: faxes and cellular phones mean people can always contact us; television brings entertainment but also news, education, exposés and frequent sales pitches. Hoardings scream messages at us, almost every shop and public place has background music. There are magazines for every conceivable and inconceivable topic. It's not enough to go to a film – you're expected to have read the reviews (in the plural) and know enough about the director/leading actors/book/plot/history . . . to be able to hold a (sensible?) discussion on it. It's no longer enough to say 'I enjoyed it – it was a good night out.'

Information anxiety and overload can occur independently, but often occur together, and they can lead to time-wasting on a massive scale. Not only is there all the time spent collecting the information, it has to be processed, sifted, sorted, stored (physically and mentally) and can contribute to procrastination, particularly in decision-making.

You have a problem with information overload if you:

- Feel anxious that you don't know everything about a topic
- Spend more time collecting information than processing it
- See the end point as *having* the information rather than understanding it – you own the article but you haven't read it
- You use phrases/jargon you don't really understand
- You feel constantly guilty about what you haven't read/don't know

- You can't separate core information or key concepts from peripheral ideas
- You get bored very quickly and need new 'input' all the time – if it's not exciting, it's boring
- You feel anxious/guilty when you don't know something
- You don't recognize information pollution, e.g. junk mail

Why are people so anxious to have information?

Information as Anxiety-Reducing

Searching for new information becomes a way of reducing anxiety. Your concern is that by not knowing something you will make a wrong decision and this would be awful. Information gathering becomes a 'legitimate' way to procrastinate and may be linked to perfectionism (see Chapter 7). You're looking for the right answer, which only shows itself when you have collected all the information there is.

Information as Status

Your underlying concern is that by not knowing something you will look ignorant/stupid/old fashioned/out of touch and this would be awful. Information, or rather, the ability to stay on top of information has a status all of its on. We admire people who are experts in their field, and use it to get ahead. Even more we admire people who are knowledgeable in many areas. When Jacob Bronowski presented *The Ascent of Man* we were captivated by the man as well as the subject. Here was someone who could expound knowledgeably on a wide variety of disciplines and topics, and make it comprehensible to the lay person.

The concept of Renaissance man was a reality in the Renaissance as it was possible then to have a working knowledge of the different sciences, arts, philosophy and religion. But the increase in our understanding of the universe during the last 400 years, through

science, art, philosophy and technology, has made the idea of knowing
or understanding everything laughable.

If you see knowledge as power/status you may hoard it (even after
it is out-of-date) and not want to share it. If other people know
something you can't make use of it. Thus you identify knowledge as
that which nobody else knows.

Information as Sensation

So much information comes at you that you start to define this as
normal and thus no new information gets defined as abnormal. This
is seen either as worrying or boring. If it's worrying you're probably
in the information-as-anxiety-reducing group. If something ceases to
interest you once you understand it, if you want constant change and
new things then you're likely to be responding to a need for
information as a source of stimulation to keep you hyped-up. Such
a person craves more and more information and never feels satisfied.

Managing Information

- Accept that you can't know/understand everything – and find
  ways to deal with your underlying unrealistic expectations of
  knowledge in relation to anxiety/status/ sensation.
- Recognise that knowing where to get up-to-date information is,
  in most cases, as good as having the information yourself.
- Learn to separate core information from peripheral
  information – when time is short read only what is essential to
  get the job done.
- Distinguish between basic information which is worth
  remembering/storing/otherwise holding on to and information
  which will quickly become obsolete. Don't store the latter.
- Reduce guilt/anxiety about what you haven't read by throwing
  it out – books are not sacred objects, they can be dumped. Tear
  articles out of magazines and throw the remainder out.

- Cut down the time you spend gathering irrelevant information – for example, don't watch the news three times in an evening/don't read every word in the newspaper/try not reading a newspaper at all . . .
- Share information gathering – several people working together can divide the task up and provide résumés/précis for others.
- Practise saying 'Can you explain that' and 'I don't know' rather than dumbly nodding your head. It's all right not to know.
- Get taken off mailing lists for junk/irrelevant mail.

12

MEETINGS

When shall we three meet again
In thunder, lightning, or in rain?
WILLIAM SHAKESPEARE

It is a truth universally acknowledged that anyone with not enough time goes to too many meetings. Meetings are a waste of time, accomplish little, are frustrating, boring, happen too often, at inconvenient times and last too long. Everyone hates meetings. Right?

Most people fall into this category, but there are those who, even if they agree with some of the above, can't bear to miss out on a meeting. They seem to live by the philosophy 'I meet therefore I am.' And it is such people who arrange the many meetings the rest of us try to avoid. They delight in the nuances of executives, sub-committees, sub-groups, forums, divisions and sub-divisions; the differences between decision-making meetings for action and decision-making for policy, brainstorming and opinion-gathering groups and meetings to persuade others to their point of view. Meetings have become, for such people, a way of defining themselves and their importance. Often the purpose of the meeting for them is less to get something done, but to have it seen to be done. They're likely to waste a lot of everyone's time dealing with tasks with individuals which could more easily, and more properly, be done privately. They just want to be seen to be involved/make decisions/working. Such behaviour is often accompanied by working long hours in the workplace and carrying enormous mounds of work home in several briefcases/carrier bags/suitcases. With such a person for a boss the need to understand the workings of meetings is even more important.

If you are such a person then you need to start by questioning why you are so devoted to meetings.

Types of Meetings

> *Great things are done when men and mountains meet:*
> *This is not done by jostling in the street.*
>
> WILLIAM BLAKE

On the whole, when we speak of meetings, we are referring to groups of between about four and twelve people. Beyond that size they start to get unwieldy, but that doesn't stop bigger meetings/committees existing. In most cases, however, the bulk of the work is carried out in smaller groups – sub-committees. Meetings can be formal or informal, happen regularly or irregularly, frequently or rarely. People attend willingly or unwillingly with varying degrees and types of motivation. The following comments apply as much to board meetings as church councils, department working parties to parent/teacher associations.

If we only think of meetings as a number of people gathered together we overlook the large number of meetings going on everyday, formally and informally, between two people. Three or more people does not guarantee that the business being discussed is any more important than when there are two. The same principles hold for a meeting with one other person as they do with a group of people.

Why Hold Meetings?

Some meetings are held because it's 10 a.m. on Tuesday and there is always a heads of departments meeting then – whether there's anything to discuss or not. Annual General Meetings are held to comply with constitutions. *Ad hoc* groups come together to deal with a particular issue. Planning meetings are held, ostensibly to plan . . .

but we've all attended meetings where the objective is more to obstruct than to plan, to rubber stamp rather than discuss and decide. When asking what the purpose of any meeting is (whether it's one you're chairing or one you're attending) you need to bear three separate reasons in mind:

1. The formal reason or agenda
2. The hidden agenda
3. Your agenda

1. The formal reason will be laid out clearly for all to see in the form of an agenda, and will include issues for discussion, information and decision-making. Agenda setting will be discussed later.
2. The hidden agenda will depend on a variety of factors, not least the type of meeting and who is organizing it. It may include being seen to be democratic, being seen to work, to fulfil social or team building needs and so on. Functions of meetings are discussed below.
3. Your agenda may be as basic as being seen to be there/to be co-operative/to show willing to your boss or whoever has told you to go/to be seen by others to be involved/to bring yourself to the notice of others/to take part in the decision-making process/to see the decision-making process at work/to keep yourself updated, involved . . . Your reasons may be more or less elaborate and if you are not to waste your time it is important to be clear about:

   • What your objectives in attending the meeting are
   • What the likelihood of your achieving them is
   • What would happen if you didn't go

Never attend a meeting without knowing what you want to get out of it.

Functions of Meetings

We tend to think of meetings as decision-making or policy-shaping groups, but there are many more functions of a meeting than that.

These functions may or may not be appropriate – that is, they may be useful or waste time:

- Meetings define the team. The group/team/unit is defined by the people who attend. The sense of 'in-group' is developed and thus creates an 'out-group' – those who are not there. In some situations the meeting is the only time the group/team/unit/department comes together as a whole and thus is necessary if any sense of unity is to exist. For there to be group loyalty or solidarity then the group must be seen to exist. You see where you fit into the department/team/company/process and also where others fit in.
- The meeting allows the manager/head of department/supervisor or whoever to be seen as a leader rather than simply a boss to whom individuals report.
- Meeting as a group helps individuals understand what the collective aim/goal of the group is. It enables them to see how they fit into the wider picture of the group and to evaluate their, and others', contribution in view of the group's stated aims.
- A meeting helps create commitment to decisions made by members of the meeting. This is partly because being party to the decision-making process makes the individual aware of how and why the decision was reached and realize that it is not arbitrary. Team spirit or in-group feelings are strengthened and this encourages commitment to the group objectives.
- A meeting can be an information exchange, not only for individual members, but it updates and revises what is known as a group.
- A (small) meeting may generate more ideas/solutions (for example, through brainstorming) than one person alone. It can become a creative forum. To be worthwhile the group must work beyond the abilities of its most creative individual.
- Meetings are the place for democracy to work, where joint decisions are taken over policy, planning, long and short-term action.
- Meetings are arenas for displays of status in all its forms, ranging

from formal leadership to one-upmanship, demonstrations of allegiance to material symbols of status.

- Meetings can be used to motivate people, bringing together aspects of team building, commitment and socialization with new ideas and plans.
- Meetings can be used to dilute authority or responsibility by a manager/department head/decision-maker who is uncomfortable with their role or the decision they have to take. By making the decision the responsibility of the group they are let off the personal hook.
- Meetings can delay decision-making – by simply putting it off to the next meeting, because a crucial person isn't there, by demanding agreement from disagreeing parties, by talking it out of time so no decision is made, by going over the same ground until people get bored and give up . . .
- Social needs can be fulfilled at meetings. Beyond the team strengthening aspects they break up a day, bring people into contact with others they rarely see, introduce people to others in the same organization, allow for a period of chatting before and after (preferably not during), provide interaction with other for people who work alone.
- Meetings can be a security blanket. If-it's-the-departmental-meeting-it-must-be-Tuesday-morning is not very helpful, but in times of change/management turnover/restructuring the very regularity of routine meetings can be a stable base to exchange information/opinions/rumours and offer mutual support and reinforcement.

Before you say a meeting is a waste of time consider the above list and consider whether the meeting has some purpose after all. It is unrealistic to assume that every meeting you attend will take earth-shattering decisions and if this is what you expect you will inevitably be disappointed. A broader approach to what you want to get out of the meeting means you can make more realistic decisions about how important it is you attend. If, for example, you decide that your main reason for going is to 'show willing' and establish yourself as part of the group, then you might decide attending two out of three, or even two out of four meetings is sufficient. If you're fighting to defend your territory or resources you may decide you always need to be there. If you attend a large meeting where the bulk of the work is done in sub-committees you will feel less frustrated if you accept that than if you expect/want every issue to be debated fully in a group of upwards of forty people. You may decide you get enough information simply from reading the minutes.

Organizing Meetings

Objectives

Decide what these are before any other aspects of arranging a meeting. What is the purpose of the meeting?

- Informative: to update people, give and receive progress reports, to discuss issues in a general (often vague) way
- Innovative: to consider the future, in terms of new policy/strategy/projects/products/processes
- Action: decision-making about how best to proceed, or how best to implement decisions taken elsewhere
- Persuasion: to convert people to a point of view/decision taken elsewhere, to persuade people so as to reach a consensus
- To form a formal framework for innovation and action
- To socialize
- Habit!

Could the objectives be achieved in another way? Information can be circulated and announcements made in a memo. If *you* are making the decision, rather than a consensus, is it better to gather information/opinions individually? If the meeting is nothing more than updating and status reports can this be handled by a telephone conference? This is also a useful option when people are scattered across the country as it saves time and money, it also makes setting a date easier. People can find time in the day for a telephone conference when they couldn't spend half a day travelling to a meeting. It also cuts down on the time people chatter.

Timing

- Frequency: Avoid too many meetings, but if you're in a phase of rapid change/decision-making you need them frequently enough so that decisions can be made/people don't get out of touch.
- Schedule regular meetings at the same time or set dates well in advance so people can plan their diary around them, or not, as the case may be.
- The most productive meetings last under an hour, but meetings often stretch on and on. One and a half hours is probably realistic. If you regularly have very long meetings consider whether two shorter ones would be more productive, particularly if not everyone has to be there for all items. Do all the agenda items need to be there? Every time? Sometimes a long meeting is needed to get over the hump of reiterating the same old issues and to move forward (although a good chairperson should be able to do this). This may be true when discussing future policy/planning and a wide, general discussion is needed. It should, however, be used sparingly.
- Meetings held an hour before lunch or at the end of the working day are more likely to keep to time.
- People are more likely to be alert first thing in the morning, sleepy after lunch and tired and/or irritable at the end of the day.
- Don't keep cancelling meetings and rearranging dates to suit people's changing commitments. Encourage people to make their own decisions on the priority of the meeting. If they continually decide other things are more important they shouldn't complain about being left out (see below).

- If you schedule meetings over meals be certain that the food isn't going to distract people from the purpose of the meeting and that the topic, combined with eating, isn't going to give you indigestion.

People

- The less people the faster and easier (usually) business progresses. The definition of the most functional committee, one with three people, two of whom never attend, holds true in many cases.
- Have the people there who are necessary for the objectives of the meeting; for example, people who know what is going on and people who have the authority to make decisions. Often heads of departments attend, but know less about the project than those lower down the hierarchy who are actually involved. Either get these people involved with (limited) decision-making authority or devise ways that heads of departments actually know enough about what is going on to contribute. Another overlooked group are those who are going to have to implement the decisions.
- If necessary, invite people for part of a meeting, to contribute 'expert opinion' on an agenda item.
- For analysis and decision-making meetings the best numbers are between six and eight people.
- Resist the urge to invite/exclude people for political (or even personal) reasons (unless you're planning a palace revolution)
- If someone vital to the decision-making process can't be there reschedule. If one person keeps doing this see if you can get the information/authority another way or point out decisions will be made without them. Not coming to meetings can be used as a delaying tactic for all sorts of reasons.

Place

- This should be somewhere convenient to participants, which means that it should be easy to get to. Consider also factors such as ventilation, temperature, outside noise.
- Find a room of suitable size. Big enough for large groups but not overwhelming for three or four people.
- Are there suitable facilities, such as overhead projectors, flip charts, if these are deemed necessary?
- Is it away from distractions? For a long meeting to discuss policy/strategy try going away from the department/company for half a day or a day.

Procedure

- Send the agenda out in sufficient time (about three to five days) to allow people to think about issues/canvass opinions/gather data together/research background information.
- Start on time – no matter who is missing.
- Finish on time – only allow meetings to overrun in exceptional circumstances, i.e. when there are an unusual number of important/urgent issues and not because people have been waffling away from the point.
- Have a 'good' agenda (see below) and stick to it.
- Don't allow time for reading papers which should have been read prior to the meeting – this penalizes those who have done their homework.
- Be clear about who is taking the minutes.
- Ask what people want to raise under AOB (any other business) so that time can be allowed for them.
- Allow sufficient time for difficult or controversial topics.
- It takes skill to put times by each agenda item, both in terms of chairing and experience in how long items will last, what the level of discussion will be and so on. It can encourage people to talk more – either to make sure something takes as long as

suggested or, if they want to be difficult, so the item runs out of time and they can say they were prevented from making their point. You may, however, want to give some indication, either by suggesting five minutes by some items or 'major' by items you expect to take the longest time/are the most important.

- If you're inviting people to the meeting either see them first or set a time and stick to that one, timed item.
- Don't allow people to dodge backwards and forwards on the agenda.
- Briefly review decisions made/action to be taken/points made in discussion as each topic is crossed off the agenda to make sure that everyone understands/agrees.
- Use appropriate techniques – everything from brainstorming to handouts of relevant figures or use visual aids, such as overhead projectors.
- Don't allow distractions/interruptions (e.g. phone messages) unless they are a genuine emergency.
- If it's a long meeting have a break.
- Coffee/refreshments available throughout keeps a meeting informal but can add to the time. Coffee before/after allows people time for their chatting.
- Unless everyone smokes don't allow smoking. It is better for everyone's health, keeps non-smokers happy and encourages smokers to keep up the pace of the meeting so they can finish and get to their cigarette.
- Decide how people who can't attend may be allowed to contribute – send a deputy, send a written report/information/opinions or ask someone to speak on their behalf.
- Some people suggest 'stand-up meetings'. With no chairs people will get to the point and stay there. This may be useful for shortish meetings, but not where you expect a lengthy discussion or where people have to juggle sets of papers. Nor where feelings run high: people may express more aggression standing up and a table between them may provide a useful barrier!
- Try to finish on an optimistic or unifying note, or, at the very

least, not with controversy and when people are annoyed with one another.

Follow-up

- Minutes should be circulated fairly quickly after the meeting and include:
  - Information, relevant points of discussion
  - Decisions taken
  - Actions to be taken, by whom and with deadlines
- Minutes should be circulated to everyone at the meeting and those who should have been there.
- If there is relevant information for other people this might be better sent as an appropriate memo rather than in the form of the minutes of a meeting they don't attend, and don't know necessarily why they've received them. Or highlight the relevant points of the minutes and draw their attention to it with a note.

Agenda

- State starting and finishing times.
- Items should be defined, rather than broad subject headings. This may necessitate a number of sub-headings under each topic but means that people know what is meant.
- Label items for information, for discussion or action.
- Start with something easy or non-controversial to get people going, allow people to think something has been achieved, allow for latecomers, get people over their attention lag and unite them – then move into more problematic areas. People will be more alert/lively/creative early on and more fed up/bored/argumentative later, so you need to take advantage of this.
- Within this framework, order agenda items on grounds of urgency and importance.

- Put names beside agenda items if they are the responsibility of certain people.
- If people are to contribute special information, remind them of this (either on the agenda or on a note with it).

The agenda is a bit like a plan drawn up for a trip. It can either get you from A to B quickly, briefly visiting only the places you have to go to, or it can allow time for the scenic route, uncovering who knows what on the way.

Chairing Meetings

They be blind leaders of the blind. And if the blind lead the blind, both shall fall into the ditch.

MATTHEW 15.14

The chairperson in a meeting has a number of functions. They will be responsible for the procedure of the meeting and probably for the agenda, both covered above. Other aspects of chairing meetings include:

- To keep the meeting on target, to see that it keeps moving and that it achieves its objectives.
- To provide structure and control. You need to stop people jumping ahead or retreading old ground. This is best done by encouraging the presentation of relevant information, then allowing a discussion and only then moving on to decision-making and action.
- To summarize decisions taken and/or review discussion points – for clarification, as a way of dealing with the whole group arguing, but not to update latecomers.
- If absolutely necessary, to arrange for a vote.
- To check that people understand what they have to do.
- To encourage participation – be receptive and non-judgemental.

- To discourage hogging of discussion/irrelevant interruptions.
- To understand different people's roles and make appropriate use of them, whether it is the person who is always positive or the one who can spot any problem as a tiny dot on the horizon.
- To enable the group to deal with difficult people as far as possible, but, if necessary, deal with the difficult, obstructive person tactfully in the meeting. In some instances the person will have to be tackled about their role/behaviour outside the group.
- To not argue with negative people. Get opinions from the rest of the group and keep the meeting on target.
- To stop issues from becoming personal. If personal arguments break out, or people become personally insulting, stop it immediately. Suggest they take the matter up outside the meeting and bring everyone back to the agenda issue.
- Do not use meetings to show people how much work the chairperson does, or deal with matters that should be dealt with individually.

Participating in Meetings

Most of us are members of meetings more often than we chair them. Although poor meetings often result from poor chairing, ask yourself what you do which contributes to the problem and what you could do to improve it:

- Ask what you want to get out of the meeting and whether you're likely to achieve this. If you've no good reason for being there don't go. You'll probably be negative and this will affect others.
- Be considerate: be on time, don't dash in and out of meetings, don't take messages – leave your cellular phone behind.
- Take an active part, but appropriately. Don't ramble, be clear, concise, relevant.
- If you're there as a constituency representative be clear when you're speaking on their behalf or stating your own opinion.

- Don't feel you have to comment on every topic.
- If you're always negative start questioning why. Do you resent/fear change? Is it the result of low morale? Do you want to be/enjoy being difficult? Are you getting your own back on the chairperson?
- If you talk a lot question whether it's relevant/appropriate. Are you showing off your knowledge/inside information/allegiances? Is it because you're bored? Are you trying to make an impression?
- You can't do everything at once. Be selective about which important issues you will take a stand on.
- Time your contributions carefully: don't leave negative comments until the end of the discussion when everyone is ready to move on/vote/has come to a consensus.
- It helps to talk to people before the meeting and find out if you have any allies.
- If a discussion is rambling you can help the chairperson get it back on course:
  - Make a relevant contribution
  - Go back to the last relevant point made
  - Summarize/ask for a summary of the points made so far
- Lighten a tense/argumentative atmosphere if appropriate, for example, through humour.
- Be positive, pick up on other people's useful points, encourage others.
- Don't get drawn into personal arguments and don't take criticism of ideas personally.
- Offer constructive, rather than destructive criticism.
- Do your homework before the meeting so you know the ramifications of what is coming up and have your ideas thought out/relevant information to hand/know the opinions of those you represent/have answers to practical objections.
- Take your diary, so dates of other meetings can be set.
- Do what you have agreed to do after the meeting.

Cost-effectiveness of Meetings

Everyone knows how to calculate the cost of meetings by adding up the hourly rate of all participants. The cost of many meetings appears frightening and it is easy to start thinking that the cost is not worth the outcome. A couple of people, or even one, could have taken the same decision, or it could have been reached in half the time. But humans are social beings and the herd instinct is strong. Bonding, developing team spirit, increasing commitment, improving involvement and networking are all part of the meetings culture. These are things which are difficult to quantify and measure but are important for good, co-operative working and to maintain morale. One man reported that his monthly departmental meetings lasted about an hour. Even when business was conducted in less time people still sat around chatting. Wondering if they were wasting time it quickly became clear that there were reasons for this – it was the only time the core department members got together. It was interesting to note that some of the assistants wandered off back to work, but that for those who remained it was their only opportunity to update each other on what was going on in general terms, to exchange ideas and gossip. Since these people never took coffee breaks, and only irregular lunchtimes, this quarter-of-an-hour bonding session, when they were reaffirming themselves as part of the same department, with ultimately the same goals, was valuable. Such behaviour should be seen as legitimate and not a waste of fifteen minutes once a month.

PART 5

You and Time

13

TIME AND ENERGY

Old age is the most unexpected of all things which happen to a man.

LEV TROTSKY

Managing time is as much about managing energy as it is hours and minutes. We have only so much energy and although it can be increased through sensible habits, including sufficient sleep and rest, exercise and a healthy diet, it is not infinite. Gaining some control over time affects other aspects of your life. There is no point in rushing around all day in an attempt to work faster or achieve more if this leaves you exhausted at the end of the day, so that you pass out in front of the television. Even if you still have some energy left if you have nothing to do with the time you've saved you will rapidly revert to your old habits. What is to stop you? How many people protect themselves by being so busy they can say 'I never have a moment to stop and think' when, if they did have a moment, they would realize they had no thoughts worthy of the name?

Managing time and energy means taking time out for ourselves, to care for ourselves, to enjoy leisure pursuits, to value others. We all have many facets to our personalities and time needs to be found to express these different parts of ourselves.

Patterns of Energy, Patterns of Work

For blue collar workers in manufacturing industries the working week has shortened, but these are industries in decline. For industries in the ascendancy, in service industries and for people in managerial and professional occupations, the working week is getting longer and we expect more and more of ourselves. In managing your time you need to make decisions about how *long* you are going to work, as well as *how* you are going to work. Recent research has suggested that working longer than fifty to sixty hours a week becomes counterproductive, as you slow down, become less efficient and effective and make more mistakes. Using weekends and evenings to complete work not finished during the day means you never get a real break and you feel stale. If you have run out of energy by the middle of the week and struggle through Thursday and Friday, having a real break at the weekend is a better strategy so that you then have enough energy to get through the week.

'A change is as good as a rest' works for some people, or in some circumstances, at least up to a point. If you are going to work in the evenings and at weekends, try to vary what you do from what you have been doing all day. There is a psychological difference working on something in the evenings if it is your choice and it develops your skills/interests/career. Studying for further qualifications/developing your pet project/writing a book/learning a new skill/going on a weekend course is quite different from bringing home routine work that you 'should' be able to get through during the day.

There is a limit to how long you can concentrate on one task without showing some degree of performance decline – even tasks you're interested in. After about an hour you lose your edge. To be able to keep going you either have to change tasks or take a break (see below). The majority of people who say they can work on and on without stopping are naturally taking breaks but not thinking about them. The couple of minutes they take to get a drink/go to the toilet/stretch their arms don't distract from the task but provide sufficient break of concentration and change of posture to allow the task to continue. Boring tasks usually can be sustained for less time than interesting ones and require more breaks.

Larks and Owls

Most people will quickly label themselves a lark or an owl; they either enjoy getting up early and work better first thing in the morning or they can't bear early mornings but will happily stay up half the night. Your natural tendency may be constrained by the demands of your family or your job, or you feel that you have to fit into a conventional, socially appropriate pattern. Physiologists tell us there is an energy curve which is remarkably similar for everyone, with a high around mid morning (say between 10 a.m. and 12 noon), dropping off after lunch with a second rise in the curve towards the end of the afternoon. Our lowest point is around 3 a.m. Having said that, external factors will affect how you feel and act. People adapt to circumstances. If you get a surge of energy at 9 p.m. it may have as much to do with the children finally being in bed and/or chores out of the way and you now have the freedom to give your whole attention to whatever it is you want to do. There is nothing wrong with this. Getting into the habit of always working at particular times makes it very much easier to get on with things and not procrastinate.

If you're not sure when you're at your intellectual peak/have most energy keep an energy log for a while. Either keep this along with your time log or separately. Every hour, note down how you feel on a scale of 1 to 7, with 7 as your highest score and 1 as the lowest. How you define this depends on what aspects of functioning matter most to you. You may choose to rate being physically energetic or intellectually alert, but for most of us a global score which combines these makes most sense. If you keep this in conjunction with your time log you will get the most from it. If you're keeping it separately note down what you were doing at the time and/or immediately before. This enables you to look at your patterns of energy and how they are influenced by what you do.

It should come as no surprise that you feel sleepy and lethargic after a big lunch, particularly if it included alcohol. It might be more interesting, however, to note that when you work straight through lunch, either missing it altogether or eating a sandwich at your desk, you hit a real low in the mid-afternoon from which it is difficult to recover; or that working late the night before, or getting up early, means you run out of energy by 3 or 4 p.m.

Depending on circumstances you can either stay with this pattern, and do something about the mid-afternoon low, or alter the precursors of the problem. If you're going to do something about the low:

- Have lunch. If you've skipped a meal your blood sugar will drop and you'll feel tired and irritable. (Have you noticed how medics are never tired and irritable but always hypoglycaemic?)
- If you had something to eat, try fruit juice rather than coffee to wake you up. (A lunch that consisted of mainly sugar and strong coffee will raise your blood sugar quickly, but temporarily, and it will drop quickly.)
- Go for a walk. You grabbed a sandwich but have still been sitting all day without movement. It need not be long and could involve delivering messages elsewhere in the building.
- Get some fresh air. If you've been cooped up inside all day going outside the building helps – even in a city where 'fresh air' is a very loose term. If you work in an environment with no windows and no natural daylight this is likely to be especially important.
- Get some exercise. If you're really lethargic (but not lack-of-sleep tired) and your job permits it, go for a quick jog or swim.
- Take a nap – but only if you know you're tired through lack of sleep over the past couple of days, otherwise trying to sleep will only add to your problems. If you wake up feeling worse the chances are you slept for too long and thus too deeply. A ten to fifteen minute cat-nap is what you want. Cat-napping is a habit which can be learnt like any other, and it is vital for people working very long hours or who are on call and get interrupted at night.

Avoid the problem:

- Don't expect to work eighteen hours a day and never feel tired. Get enough sleep.
- Take breaks. You can't concentrate on and on. Stop what you're doing, get up and move around/make a phone call/deliver a message in person/go for a (de-caffeinated) coffee or fruit

juice/tidy your desk . . . If you're working at home you can put the washing on/peel the potatoes/wash up . . . At home or at work you could be more indulgent and have a quick look at a journal, magazine or newspaper. Be careful – you are not trying to squash even more into the time available but to have a recuperative break. A few minutes staring out of the window, daydreaming while you drink your tea/coffee/mineral water is probably the best break of all. We are, after all, talking about five minutes.

The only time to consider not taking a break (of more than a stretch of your arms) is when it was very, very hard to start, and doing anything else is better, and you are doing a difficult task but it is currently going well and you know that if you stop restarting will be hell. Stay with it while you're winning. But stop while you're ahead. Don't let it run on until it becomes awful again.

- Change your task. If you're falling asleep over your desk (due to lethargy not tiredness) do something that requires more energy. Stand, move around, go walkabout. If you're lack-of-sleep tired and you can't concentrate, try tasks that require little thought – do your filing, tidy your desk, sort out the drawer you've been shoving everything in for the past year.
- Vary boring tasks and interesting ones, easy and difficult.

Stress

It is better to wear out than rust out.
BISHOP RICHARD CUMBERLAND

One definition of stress is that there are more demands on a person than they have resources to cope with. Thus the poor time manager's cry of 'too much to do' can be seen as a potential source of stress. Some people find it easier to admit to having a problem with time management than to admit to being stressed. Indeed, many people are unable to recognize their own stress. If colleagues and, especially, close friends or family are telling you you are stressed, pay attention to them. We all tend to be blind to ourselves and believe we are coping when others can see that we are not — or are barely hanging on by the skin of our teeth.

The relationship between stress and poor time management is a chicken and egg problem. Always feeling rushed, under pressure and having too much to do contributes to being under stress. Being stressed can lead to fatigue and lethargy, having memory or concentration problems, being moody and sleeping badly, all of which contribute to inefficient and ineffective work and so add to time management problems. Stress can contribute to a wide variety of health problems from repeated colds and flu to heart disease. Sickness slows you down (possibly permanently) and thus you work less effectively and efficiently. If you are losing days off work to repeated minor infections you may well want to consider whether this is an indication of stress. Rather than hurrying back to work before you're fully fit and then working long hours to make up for lost time, you would be wiser to take enough sick leave to make sure you're over the infection and then pay special attention to your health. If you're beginning to feel unwell, act on this (get more sleep, take it easy or see your doctor if appropriate) rather than pushing on in the vain hope that if you ignore it, it will go away.

Some people only get ill at weekends and on holiday. I recently heard one woman say after a bank holiday weekend which she'd spent in bed with flu: 'At least I'm never ill on company time.' If you find yourself saying something like that consider what this is telling you about your underlying attitude to work and leisure time, and the stress that you are under.

The central issues in the development of stress have to do with uncertainty and lack of control, and time management problems echo this. Although some of the causes of stress will quite genuinely have to do with external circumstances and demands, some causes involve the way the individual perceives and experiences events.

When managing stress, like managing time, there is no one, quick, easy answer. Coping mechanisms depend both on the causes of the stress and the personality and attitudes of the individual. Like time management, coping with wider stress issues involves analysing the causes of the problem and then learning new skills, challenging old beliefs and developing new attitudes. I have covered this in a previous book, *Coping with Stress at Work* (Thorsons).

Sleep

Disruptions in our pattern of sleeping are frequently among the first signs of problems. Difficulty in getting to sleep, lying in bed wide awake with your thoughts churning, is indicative of stress, whereas waking up in the wee small hours and being unable to get back to sleep may be a symptom of depression.

Cutting down on sleep is one way of trying to create more time — you effectively lengthen the day by two hours if you only sleep six instead of eight hours. It is not, however, an appropriate solution for most of us. You can try cutting down your sleep and see how you feel, but the people who do well on five or six hours are not common. Not sleeping for eight hours became, however, a new status symbol in the 1980s. It showed you're a go-getting kind of person, 'on the fast track'. Sleep has become another of those things that is only for wimps, and if you're committed to your job you should be able to work most of the night and still feel fresh, bright and energetic the next day. This is unrealistic for most people. Many of us can 'manage' on less sleep than we'd really like, but this should only be a short-term solution.

There are some people trying to sleep too much. If you're sleeping eight-plus hours a night and still wake up feeling tired, try sleeping less and see how you feel. If you're having trouble getting to sleep/wake up early and are sure you're not stressed/depressed maybe your body is telling you you don't need so much sleep. Although elderly people need less sleep, most of us hit middle age aware that we need more sleep than we used to. It's not just the bags under our eyes that tell us we don't bounce back after a late night with the resilience of our youth; other signs are always needing to be woken by the alarm clock, always feeling worse at the end of the week than the beginning and needing to sleep late during weekends and holidays. You probably even use the phrase 'to catch up'. Women in particular may have a problem; there is some evidence to suggest career women already sleep less than men and they certainly can't sacrifice any of their sleeping time.

Sleep deprivation is cumulative, but we quickly learn to accommodate our sleepiness. It becomes defined as 'normal'. Performance and mood are both affected by sleep deprivation. We are less likely to be creative and more likely to make mistakes as the day wears on, even in routine tasks. In some jobs, ranging from long distance lorry drivers to doctors, such mistakes can have dangerous, even fatal consequences. Chronically tired people are more likely to be moody, irritable and depressed and this affects their relationships with other people as well as their job performance. If you drink a lot of coffee to stay awake your irritability may be exacerbated by caffeine-overload. Caffeine is a powerful stimulant and can make people feel jittery, anxious or hyped-up.

Taking cat-naps is one solution and best suits people who find they don't sleep long at night naturally, or whose schedule (such as being on call) forces them into less sleep than they'd like. It is not the answer, however, for the latter, in the long run, nor is it suitable for the chronically tired.

The problem lies in the loss of REM (rapid eye movement) sleep which denotes dreaming. We have REM sleep approximately every 90 minutes of sleep, but the longer we sleep the longer the REM lasts, and it peaks in the last third of a normal sleep cycle. Researchers believe that it is REM deprivation which is the real culprit, particularly for mood symptoms. Naturally short sleepers may have a sleep cycle which is contracted so they still get their REM sleep in, whereas those who are not miss this when they get up earlier than they want. Since the REM sleep is dependent on your sleep cycle it doesn't matter whether you work late or get up early, it is still the end of your sleep you loose. A few nights of good sleep will usually relieve the problem as we spend a greater proportion of our time in REM sleep to catch up. So sleeping late at the weekend is not a bad idea. If your sleep deprivation is chronic it will take several weeks of 'good' sleep to make up the loss.

There are many techniques used by insomniacs to improve their sleep and if you have a major sleep problem you should investigate these. Sleeping tablets are only ever a short-term answer because they affect the quality of the sleep (REM type) you have. If you have a minor or occasional sleep problem try any or all of the following:

- Don't go to bed after something which is mentally stimulating i.e. a violent film/the late night news/an argument with your partner or children/working/thinking about work issues . . . relax or wind down first
- Don't drink caffeine during the evening
- Don't take work to bed with you, either physically (e.g. a report to read) or mentally (e.g. a problem to think about)
- Reflect on positive issues rather than negative ones
- Find something the next day you can look forward to and concentrate on that
- Take more exercise: many sedentary workers are mentally exhausted at the end of the day but have done very little that is physical. Using your body a bit more will induce a more healthy tiredness.
- Don't cat-nap during the day: this reduces your chances of sleeping at night
- Don't spend too much time simply lying in bed
- If you're very tense then learning how to relax properly may help, not just in getting to sleep but in feeling better during the day as well

Leisure

And on the seventh day God rested – what better model could we have? Our days of rest at the weekend are losing their distinction from our Monday to Friday working days. People take work home, and some have computers and even faxes at home so the work environment as well as work itself intrudes into what should be rest.

Technology should have made work more flexible, rather it seems to have extended it. Chores take up time, shops stay open late and on Sundays. Sundays look like Saturdays and there is no incentive, no model, to slow down.

Leisure gets seen as compensation for work which is unpleasurable. 'Leisure centres' imply *planned* leisure and become tinged with work. A balance needs to be achieved in your leisure time as in all else. If you feel that every second must count, must be used productively you will try to cram more and more that you define as useful into 'free' time, when maybe you need to take time out to have fun or relax. One man who enjoyed sailing realized he had given up most of his 'sailing time' to be involved in a project teaching children to sail – worthwhile, but hard work. He had lost his own 'fun' time. The answer was to find a balance.

If you're working so hard that all you have the energy for at the end of the day is to collapse in front of the television you're unlikely to enjoy or value leisure time. If you have no hobbies, no interests, then you have no incentive to work less. To successfully cut down on the hours you work not only means working more effectively during the day, but having something worthwhile for you to do in your free time. If you are unused to 'free time', you need to plan ahead so that you won't feel anxious with this 'empty' time stretching before you.

Some people work long hours as a way of staving off boredom because they have no other interests, nothing else to do. People who are bored are usually boring as well, and the extra hours worked doesn't change this. Working long hours may be a way of denying loneliness – 'I don't have time to go out/for friends' – when, in fact, you don't have friends. Working doesn't take the place of friendship. In both cases, these are the problems which need to be tackled, along with time management.

Enjoy your leisure time:

- You will relax most with something totally different from your work. Physical activity, creativity, working with your hands rather than your head are all antidotes to sedentary or primarily thinking jobs. Or, you may use your talents in a different way. I know several surgeons who are skilled carpenters, plumbers and mechanics away from the operating theatre. The underlying enthusiasm is a combination of working with their hands and taking things apart and putting them back together (hopefully in better working order). If you're surrounded by people at work, solitude may be welcome at the weekend, or company if you work alone.

- If leaving things to chance means you do nothing, plan ahead. Season tickets for concerts, theatre and sporting events push you into going. Or get together with a group of friends so that each person/couple takes it in turns to organize a monthly outing – to the theatre, a new restaurant or whatever. Join a group or society which holds regular events.
- Make a ritual out of spending some time with the family, anything from a regular Sunday brunch out to Sunday evening with a rented video and popcorn.
- If you can't stop working at home, or can't unwind there, have a break away from home – one or two nights, with or without the children.
- Schedule breaks between projects, even a day or two. This isn't the same as not knowing what you're doing but enjoying the completion of one project before plunging headlong into the next.

Energy and the Environment

Men talk of killing time, while time quietly kills them.
DION BOUCICAULT

There are a number of issues that affect people's work habits and time management which is worth bringing to your attention, although each requires more space than is available here to deal with them properly.

Seasonal Affective Disorder

It is only fairly recently that psychiatrists have started to look seriously at the phenomenon of winter depression or seasonal affective disorder, although theories linking mood and seasonality date back to Hippocrates in Ancient Greece. Known, aptly, as SAD, seasonal affective disorder is thought to be related to the reduction in hours of daylight which suppresses the production of the hormone melatonin and is treated by supplementary sunlight. Although there is still some controversy surrounding SAD and its treatment, if you get depressed from late autumn to early spring for no apparent reason it may be worth checking this out.

If you think SAD may be a problem for you check with your doctor and try:

- Fitting full spectrum lights to simulate daylight
- Avoiding oversleeping, which will only make you feel worse
- Taking exercise, which will give you more energy
- Eating regular, sensible meals (with complex carbohydrates) to give you sustained energy
- A winter holiday in the sun!

Sick Building Syndrome

The building you work in may contribute to ill health, feelings of lethargy and tiredness as well as headaches, sore throats and other ear, nose and throat problems and skin rashes. Although there is some dispute over this, sick building syndrome is recognized by the World Health Organization which has estimated that as many as 30 per cent of buildings may be affected to some extent. Factors which contribute to the problem are:

- Air conditioning which recycles stale and possibly polluted air and reduces humidity
- Chemical pollution – everything from photocopiers to

furniture, printers to carpets may be emitting damaging chemicals, not to mention other people's cigarette smoke. New or refurnished offices may experience an upsurge in health problems as new fixtures and furnishings give off a variety of toxic fumes.

- Noise — from technology and open plan offices
- Microbiological factors — bacteria and mould may exist in the office from a variety of sources, everything from someone else's flu virus to mould growing on the jungle of office plants
- Light — lack of daylight, fluorescent lighting, windowless offices, computers that are always on, and light reflected off monitors
- Ergonomics — poorly designed work stations and repeated use of technology (see below)
- Electro-magnetic fields generated by VDUs
- Overcrowding, lack of personal space and privacy, including open plan offices

Some of this is controversial in terms of cause and effect, and many issues will be difficult to deal with as an individual and need to be taken up via health and safety officers, trades unions or staff groups. Things you may be able to do, or influence, are:

- Use an ionizer to clean dry, dusty air
- Take regular breaks from VDUs
- Avoid putting your VDU opposite a window
- Move office machinery away from desks
- Check air conditioning filters regularly
- Check office jungles for mould and, if necessary, reduce the number of plants. On the other hand, some plants might actively help clean the air: philodendrons, spider plants, bamboo palm and English ivy are the types to try for cleaner air. To show any effect you need one plant for every 100 square feet.

Repetitive Strain Injury

Poorly designed office equipment has always caused problems such as backache, a stiff neck and aching muscles in shoulders and arms, particularly for those who spend most of their time typing. The advent of computers and word processors means that more people do their own typing, but have never learnt how. Often they are working with keyboard/chair/desk at the wrong height or badly positioned. Repetitive strain injury (RSI), a currently fashionable diagnosis, was described in the 1920s as telegraphist's cramp amongst operators of Morse keys. Pain in wrists, hands and fingers may signal RSI, tendinitis or, at its most extreme, carpal tunnel syndrome (CTS). The latter is over-diagnosed and since treatment can range from rest or splints to steroid injections and even surgery it is better prevented than cured.

Although RSI is used to describe wrist problems any constantly repeated action may cause pain and ultimately damage. Among a list of occupational diseases it is possible to find exotica such as embroiderer's wrist and snooker player's finger.

To avoid RSI:

- Take regular breaks from a repetitive action. At the keyboard, stand up, walk about, stretch, flex your hand muscles, shake your wrists.
- Be sensible in the length of time you spend in any one day on one type of action – especially if it is not your usual work. Repeating any action day after day will cause problems. Some authors have reported RSI as they hurry to meet a deadline to finish writing a book, and are spending very long hours at a word processor.
- Check, and take advice on, the right height for keyboard and other equipment. The middle row of the keyboard should be at, or below, elbow height. Adjust your chair or get a desk of proper height for the computer. Having it on your normal desk, the one which is a comfortable height to work on, usually means your keyboard is too high. An EC Directive states that anyone

working at a VDU must have seats with adjustable back rests.
- Use foam wrist rests which keep your wrist in a natural, comfortable position.
- If necessary take Alexander Technique lessons to learn how to realign your body to eliminate current problems and prevent new ones. Anyone with posture problems as a result of their work, from dentists to musicians, would benefit from the Alexander Technique.

When all else fails take comfort from these words:

Here lies a poor woman who always was tired
For she lived in a place where help wasn't hired.
Her last words on earth were, Dear friends I am going
Where washing ain't done nor sweeping nor sewing,
And everything there is exact to my wishes,
For there they don't eat and there's no washing of dishes . . .
Don't mourn for me now, don't mourn for me never,
For I'm going to do nothing for ever and ever.

EPITAPH IN BUSHEY CHURCHYARD, PRE-1860

14

ON THE FUTURE

The future influences the present just as much as the past.
FRIEDRICH NIETZSCHE

As you have worked your way through this book I hope that you have come to understand your relationship with time better and that you are able to use this knowledge to effect lasting change. You will have recognized, I hope, that worrying about the past is unproductive and despite not being able to change it, it is possible to learn from it. You will be assessing your beliefs and trying to bring some rationality to bear on them. You may still be committed to the notion of 'having it all' but now accept that even within this, choices have to be made and priorities set. No matter how much you do, you have, you accomplish, this philosophy, taken to extremes, leads to some sense of disappointment and frustration, and your successes in every field will never be 100 per cent. You may accept this as the price you have to pay to remain motivated and to achieve as much as possible.

As you look at your behaviour and attitudes don't develop a whole new set of rationalizations to enable you to continue to procrastinate, be a perfectionist or whatever. Even planning is a waste of time if it is never implemented. Learn to understand what you mean when you say 'I'll do it tomorrow.' Although it is difficult to anyone other than a physicist, science fiction writer or Time Lord to think of time as anything other than infinite and progressing in a straight line, we do acknowledge that psychologically time is not always straightforward.

Tomorrow is . . .

immediate –

when you're putting something unpleasant off (like root canal treatment) . . .

forever –
when you're 4 years old and waiting for Santa Claus to come . . .

never –
when it's when you're going to start your diet . . .

eternity –
when you're dying today and the miracle cure will be discovered tomorrow . . .

Tomorrow can be positive, when it is part of your plan, when you have a strategy which you put into practice and it leads you nearer your goals. Goals which you have chosen, which you see yourself approaching and which you finally achieve are motivating. Feeling free to take the time to enjoy those goals, the sense of achievement, is even more motivating. As you put your new time management philosophy and techniques into practice try not to become obsessive about it and lose out on life's small pleasures. Time management is about doing what *you* want to do. It is not for me to set your priorities for you. By all means set goals of advancement, achievement, productivity, but don't lose sight of caring for others and caring for yourself.

> *Lives of great men all remind us*
> *We can make our lives sublime,*
> *And, departing, leave behind us,*
> *Footprints on the sands of time*
> HENRY WADSWORTH LONGFELLOW

FURTHER READING

Argyle, M., *Bodily Communication*, London, Routledge, 1988

Aslett, D., *Freedom From Clutter*, London, Exley, 1985

Bach, K. and Bach, B., *Assertiveness at Work*, London, McGraw Hill, 1990

Barlow, W., *The Alexander Principle*, London, Arrow Books, 1979

Burka, J. B. and Yuen, L. M., *Procrastination*, Reading MA, Addison Wesley, 1983

Fassel, D., *Working Ourselves to Death*, New York, HarperCollins, 1990

Kanter, R. M., *When Giants Learn to Dance*, London, HarperCollins, 1990

Kieffer, G. D., *The Strategy of Meetings*, London, Piatkus, 1988

Montgomery, R., *The Truth About Success and Motivation*, London, Thorsons, 1988

INDEX